THE BIG B·E·A·R BOOK

Dee Hockenberry
PHOTOGRAPHY BY Tom Hockenberry

Schiffer Publishing Ltd

77 Lower Valley Road, Atglen, PA 19310

FOR MY SISTER TRISS
AND IN LOVING MEMORY
OF OUR BELOVED
BROTHER DAVID

Printed in Hong Kong
ISBN: 0-7643-0123-3
Book Design by Audrey L. Whiteside

Library of Congress Cataloging-in-Publication Data

Hockenberry, Dee.
    The big b-e-a-r book/Dee Hockenberry; photography by Tom Hockenberry.
        p.   cm.
    Includes bibliographical references and index.
    ISBN 0-7643-0123-3 (hardcover)
    1. Teddy bears. 2. Teddy bear makers. I. Hockenberry, Tom. II. Title.
NK8740.H613   1996
    688.7'24--dc20   96-20447
                                                      CIP

Published by Schiffer Publishing, Ltd.
77 Lower Valley Road
Atglen, PA 19310
Phone: (610) 593-1777
Please write for a free catalog.
This book may be purchased from the publisher.
Please include $2.95 for shipping.
Try your bookstore first.

We are interested in hearing from authors
with book ideas on related subjects.

CONTENTS

ACKNOWLEDGMENTS

I owe a special thank you and a debt of gratitude to the following people:

To my editor and publisher, Nancy Schiffer, for her continuing support, and also to Dawn Stoltzfus at Schiffer Publishing.

To the following collectors, artists, and companies who graciously allowed me to use their teddies; thereby making this book special.

Stephen Beaumont of Gabrielle Designs Limited, George Black of the Naples Museum, Kaylee and Jeff of Beaver Valley Bears, Alice Channing, David Douglass, Margaret and Gerry Grey, Donna McPherson, Gail Norris, Ian Pout, Susan Stanton-Reid, Lin and Jon Van Houten, Jeanette Warner, Christina Wemmit-Pauk, David Worland, and Ken Yenke.

I am sincerely grateful to Leyla Maniera of Christie's, London for her swift and warmhearted response to my requests.

Hugs to Wanda Hollenbeck, for her expert proofreading on my original handwritten manuscripts.

To my husband, Tom, for his many hours of photography and computer work necessary for the completion of the manuscript.

If I have forgotten anyone please forgive me.

This book contains several Winnie the Pooh bears. The copyrights for all the Disney versions of Pooh are owned by the Walt Disney Company.

INTRODUCTION

THE TWO TEDDIES

When President William McKinley was assassinated in 1901, Vice-President Theodore Roosevelt became the 26th president of the United States. Because of his new position, the every move of this colorful figure was widely reported. Public officials inevitably become the butt of political cartoonists, and Roosevelt provided ample grist for the mill. Books extolling his famous hunting expeditions and African safaris had been published in great numbers and the historic saga of his rough riders at San Juan Hill was legendary.

It was, however, a bear hunt in his own country that became not only his most famous adventure but forever more impacted the collecting world. In 1902 Mr. Roosevelt and his hunting party traveled to Mississippi in pursuit of black bear. Unfortunately the president did not get a shot, although he was often on the trail of a bruin. Finally, in an effort to aid him, his guides captured a bear, tied it to a tree and offered the "trophy" to Roosevelt. Of course, as a sportsman, he refused to shoot what was actually a tired old specimen, but later became represented as a young cub. The incident was reported via a cartoon drawn by Clifford Berryman in the *Washington Post*. The first drawing, now buried and pretty much forgotten, did indeed depict an old ursine. A subsequent version pictures a young and frightened creature and it is this second cartoon the collector recognizes. "Drawing The Line In Mississippi" is characterized in nearly every bear book, so it is fairly safe to say it is the most famous caricature in the world.

Berryman cartoon "Drawing The Line In Mississippi."

It is surprising to note that although from this time on bears as toys rapidly took flight, it wasn't until eighty-four years later that a teddy was made to emulate Berryman's conception. Upon the suggestion of Linda Mullins, well recognized in the bear community, the Steiff company in Germany accepted the challenge and the Berryman bear became a reality.

The process of how the concept of a teddy bear starts as a germ in the brain cells, through to its emergence in final form, is a fascinating story in itself. Occasionally a first attempt may be acceptable, but as a general rule it is try, try again.

The first Steiff Berryman Bear prototype.

The second Steiff Berryman Bear prototype.

Berryman Bear prototype in small size never released.

The finished and released Berryman Bear.

The first prototype of this Berryman bear was hand made under the supervision of Jörg Juninger, director of Steiff's design center. However, on final inspection, the eyes did not meet the company's specifications and should have had off-center pupils. Additional changes that were made included replacing the tan of the face with white mohair; revising the mouth and accents; and using slimmer body parts. Though even this was not the final example, the modified prototype was used in the catalog because it was the only sample available at the time of printing. A second prototype (also under Mr. Juninger's supervision) needed further modifications as well. The firm was still experiencing difficulties finding a source for side glancing eyes, so the orbs on this specimen were hand colored. The body, arms, and legs were still too plump, and the head was deemed to be a little large for correct proportions.

Finally a Berryman Bear was finished and released in 1987. Standing 13.75 inches tall, the teddy is made of brown mohair with a white mohair face and hand airbrushed mouth and paw pad designs. The white eyes have the signature side glancing pupils and this teddy is indeed a remarkable re-creation. It was fascinating to discover that another size was also contemplated. A unique little bruin of 10.25 inches was developed, and although quite charming, it was never put into production.

Steiff Bear: 15" 1902-1903; apricot mohair; shoe button eyes; sealing wax nose; tan twine mouth; joined by metal rods; hard stuffed body; elephant button; $15,000+.
Steiff Bear: 15" 1904-1905; cinnamon mohair; shoe button eyes; side pushed squeaker; $3,500-$4,000.

The first Teddy Bears that appeared on the market after "Drawing The Line In Mississippi" (which drew attention to our four footed friends) were made at about the same time in both America and Germany. In Giengen, Germany, Richard Steiff, nephew of the firm's founder Margarete, was the chief designer. Steiff toy animals were always extremely lifelike and to achieve this realism Richard spent much time sketching the bears and animals at the Stuttgart Zoo. In the fall of 1902 he dreamed of a bear whose head and legs could move freely, and by the spring of 1903, such a creature made its debut at the Leipzig Toy Fair. The initial articulation involved the use of string, but the only bear that has surfaced in this "first" teddy bear design has metal rods as the internal mechanism. This Teddy, now referred to as a *rod bear*, looks like a living bear when placed on all four feet. The head is small, the body is hard to the touch, and the features are different from later (even by one year) products. It has the standard shoe button eyes, but the nose is sealing wax and the mouth is tan twine. Rod bears are extremely rare and realize many thousands of dollars when offered for sale.

Opposite: The first two Steiff bears showing how different their faces are.

Meanwhile, back in New York City, shopkeepers Rose and Morris Michtom were enchanted by the Roosevelt/Berryman tale. Rose's nimble fingers went to work with needle and thread, and lo and behold, a bear emerged and was placed in their store window with a sign reading "Teddy's Bear." Mr. Ted sold immediately and orders were taken for more. When demand overtook the Michtoms' ability to produce, the Ideal Toy Corporation was founded. Because early Ideal bears were not marked in a permanent manner, identification may be gleaned by studying ads in old *Playthings* magazines and from the example residing in the Smithsonian Institution.

It is obvious that the man and the bear cannot be separated. An undocumented story involves Roosevelt looking at a teddy and remarking in his jocular way that even as a so called "bear expert," he couldn't identify the breed. At this point a man exclaimed "Why, it's a *Teddy Bear* of course." A charming tale whether it is true or not.

Brochure printed in conjunction with a parade in Giengen on the occasion of Roosevelt's 100th birthday; a festival and parade was held in which a life size horse and figure of T. R. was the main attraction.

American Ideal Bear: 10" ca. 1908; gold mohair; shoe button eyes; no ID; $900-$1,000

Evidently the President approved of the association, for teddies were used extensively during his campaign for re-election. They materialized on countless political mementos. He gave them as gifts, threw them from the train on his whistle stop tours, and even decorated banquet tables with them.

American Bear: 20" ca. 1907; mohair head, paws and feet; glass eyes; tan cotton twill body fabric under clothes is the same fabric as the uniform; rough rider design with brass buttons and leather belt; $1,400-$1,700; sits astride a 36" example of the Steiff horse seen in the brochure and used in the parade.

Postcard available at the president's home in Oyster Bay, Long Island; the original portrait hangs at Sagamore Hill.

Historic "Sagamore Hill," Long Island, N.Y.   *Color Photo by Milt Price*

Roosevelt Campaign Bear: 4.50" ca. 1904; plush over bendable wire; shown with campaign button; $350-$450.

From the very beginning, Roosevelt's influence affected commercial bear products. Berryman continued to use the bear he originated in untold numbers of additional cartoons and other artists rendered their own version of Teddy Bears. Patterns for Teddy apparel inevitably included a rough rider ensemble along with everyday costumes. Books abounded, of course, the most famous being Seymour Eaton's four tomes and ten abridged versions of *The Roosevelt Bears*. Off-shoot memorabilia taken from these volumes appeared with regularity and are even more collectible today. Some American firms also issued bears dressed in rough rider regalia, since that is the costume most frequently identified with the President. Right up to the present day, both commercial and artist renditions show the alliance of this man and his bear.

Campaign postcard for Taft introducing the weasel and bidding "Teddy" farewell.

Teddy "B" and Teddy "G" 1980s; designed and distributed by D &D Productions; made for them by Dean's of England; $350-$375 ea.

Above: Teddy Roosevelt Doll and Bear: 8" 1983; hard plastic doll and flocked bear; made by Nisbet of England (now out of business.) $200-$225.

Top Right: Teddy And The Bear: 7" 1992; by artist Gladys Boalt; painted muslin; ultra suede clothes; $50-$60.

Right: Roosevelt Bear: 13" 1993; made by the Toy Works for the Adirondack Chamber of Commerce; $95-$110.

Tweed Roosevelt, great-grandson of Theodore, shown signing a "Teddy" bear at the Steiff Festival in Toledo in 1994.

Photograph of three Roosevelt Bears designed and executed by artist Beverly White; 1990s; limited editions; 30" $2,000 each.

Teddy Roosevelt
Bear; 5" 1990s; de-
signed and executed
by Canadian artist
Trudy Yelland; gift to
author.

Roosevelt Rough
Rider: 15" 1990s;
made by artist
Beverly White in a
limited edition;
poseable lock line
construction; $500-
$550.

Steiff Teddy Roosevelt
Bear: 7.50" 1994;
made for the 9th Steiff
Festival hosted by the
Toy Store in Toledo,
Ohio.

Roosevelt Bear: 15"
1994; made by author
in mohair with pearl
teeth; felt clothes
forms body; $295.

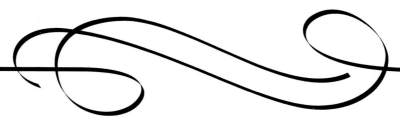

CHAPTER I
WHO'S WHO IN BEARMAKING

GERMANY

MARGARETE STEIFF GMBH.

From the company's beginning in the 1880s, the name Steiff has stood for quality in children's playthings. Margarete, the founder of Steiff, never married and thus has no direct descendants. Her nephews, however, were an integral part of the organization, and as their progeny carries on the tradition, Steiff remains a family business. Jörg Juninger, a great-grand nephew, is currently the chief designer and director of the museum and archives. He is also the goodwill ambassador and makes many visits each year to the United States.

The trademark "Knopf Im Ohr" (button in ear) is undoubtedly the most famous logo in the toy business. Until the late 1970s this button was silver in color, but the imprint on it changed over the years. Although it has always been placed in the left ear, the method of attachment has undergone some revisions. At first the button was affixed by prongs, then by a rivet, and when the color became brass in 1977, the method of riveting also underwent a new design. The following is a history of the different button imprints.

Large bronze monument at the entrance of the Steiff works in Giengen, Germany.

1904/1905-	embossed elephant with upright trunk
1905/1909-	blank button
1905/1940-	"Steiff " printed with trailing final F
1946/1947-	dull bluish silver blank button
1948/1960s-	"Steiff" in raised script
1960s/1976-	"Steiff" in incised script
1977 on-	brass button with "Steiff" in incised script

The issue of unequivocally dating a toy by the button alone is somewhat clouded, since buttons left over from a previous period are sometimes used on the bears.

A white stock tag behind the button was in use from around 1908 until 1925. For the next eight years the tag color was orange/red and about 1933 the current yellow came into vogue. Replicas and limited editions usually are issued with the early white color tag to differentiate between those and open stock products.

Steiff worker stuffing excelsior in a studio bear.

Attaching the button in the ear at the Steiff factory.

Chest tags first appeared on bears in 1926. Until 1928 they were white paper circles rimmed in metal. From 1928 until 1972 the logo became a red rimmed white paper tag with a yellow teddy head at the bottom. Even the bear's head underwent a few changes that can be noted by studying examples that still retain them. In 1972 the tag became split in color with a red bottom and a yellow top.

In September of 1994 nine dedicated collectors, including the author, were fortunate enough to have the opportunity to visit the Steiff factory. This group was traveling under the aegis of Beth and Ben Savino owners of the Toy Store and Steiff Festival promoters. Previously, selected groups were often given private escorted tours. By 1994, however, these tours had reached the point of being disruptive to the workers so regrettably our entourage was the last to have this privilege. We will always be grateful to Jörg and the other directors who entertained us so royally and enabled us to experience the full Steiff life.

GEBR. BING

Bing made their first teddy ca. 1906. Besides traditional bruins, the company was particularly known for superb clockwork and mechanical toys. The initial Bing logo was a metal clip in the ear imprinted G.B.N. (Gebr. Bing Nürnberg) but finding a bear with a clip is rather rare. You are more apt to come across a bear with a button on the side under the arm. Until 1919 this button also was labeled G.B.N. and from then until the cessation of business in 1932 the initials were simply B.W. for Bing Werke.

GEBR. SÜSSENGUTH

As far as can be determined, Süssenguth had a relatively short life span. A few pre-1920 examples have surfaced, but the most well known is *Peter*, the rather fierce specimen that was discovered in the 1970s in a German factory. The 100 or so bears were all mint in boxes and in two sizes. A limited amount were fashioned of apricot mohair and measured 17 inches. The balance, 14 inches tall , was either brown or black tipped mohair. *Peter's* eyes move from side to side in conjunction with his tongue in the open mouth. Peter Bull, the father of the adult bear movement, owned a *Peter* bear but finally gave it away because he said it scared his other bears.

WILHELM STRUNZ

This is one of the companies that plagiarized Steiff in the pre-1910 years. They dismembered products to determine jointing methods and even constructed a "rod bear." Strunz often used articulation structures that were visible from the outside. I know of no labels (if they used them) that have remained intact.

SCHUCO

In 1912 Heinrich Müller and Heinrich Schreyer began doing business in Nürnberg under the trade name of Schuco. Mechanical novelties proved to be their forte, possibly as a result of Müller's former association with Bing. Unfortunately, the partnership's rapid success was interrupted by the first World War. Both men were inducted into military service and so all production ceased.

At the war's end Schreyer left the company and Müller found a new beginning with Adolph Kahn, an energetic business man. This new team rose to even greater heights and by the mid 1920s their most enduring fabrications emerged. Best loved is the bear called "Tricky," whose head nods yes or shakes no by

tail leverage. Bright gold was the color most frequently used, but other vibrant hues do appear on occasion. They include a brilliant blue and tipped furs in vermilion, green and purple. *Teddy Messenger,* most often referred to as a bellhop, is also a popular favorite. Schuco was one of the first firms to consider the adult market. Perfume bottles and compact shaped bears, clearly meant to be carried in a flapper's purse, are even more in demand today.

Folded paper tags hung from the chest in the 1920s and by post World War II this tag changed to a red plastic affixed by a red bow. Metal wheeled bears normally have *Schuco* embossed on the wheels.

During the 1950s Schuco seemed to gain momentum. A decade later, however, the stock featured less complex ideas, probably in a effort to cut costs and remain competitive. Schuco had suffered many business reverses over the years and finally could not forestall the inevitable. In 1976 they were forced to close their doors, but recently new owners have bought the remains of the business, including the patterns, and are producing bears under the Schuco label.

GEBR. HERMANN K. G.

The Hermann family has been in the business of making teddies since 1913. Bernhard Hermann began his industry in Sonnenberg, Thuringia, an area known for toy making. In 1948 two of his four sons, Artur and Werner, set up a new Hermann enterprise in Hirschaid, a small community near the fascinating town of Bamberg. Presently the helm is held by Werner's daughter Marion Mehling and Artur's daughter Margit Drolshager. Another daughter of Artur, Traudel, is the chief designer.

The Hermann factory in Hirschaid, Germany.

On the same German journey in 1994 our touring group was greeted at the factory and delighted with the hospitality shown us by the Hermann ladies. Although we did not view the inner production workings, we had tea in the boardroom and feasted our eyes on the display of teddies, not to mention loading our suitcases with them.

The Hermanns believe in good company/customer relations. To this end they travel extensively and are always available to talk about their products and discuss labeling methods. They have included sewn-in logos as well as metal or paper hang tags. Customers often come away as charmed by the Hermanns as by their appealing bears.

Marian Hermann and the author in the boardroom.

A display of Hermann bears.

Hermann teddies on display.

HERMANN SPIELWAREN GMBH.

This company is also an offspring of the original Hermann company, run by the descendants of the other two Bernhard sons. It is affiliated, through marriage, to a member of the toy making Leven family. and they are therefore able to reproduce Leven originals. This branch has been in business since 1979 and can be identified by their labels and hang tags. Care should be taken not to confuse the two Hermann enterprises.

Kersa of Germany and Berg in Austria are still manufacturing, although Kersa no longer makes teddies. One by one, Crämer, Eli, Erle, Fechter, Helvetic, Jopi and Petz have ceased operations

UNITED STATES

THE IDEAL NOVELTY AND TOY COMPANY

This is the first company to manufacture bears in the United States. It began with Rose and Morris Michtom's single bear, which, as mentioned in the Introduction, was made as a salute to the Berryman cartoon. The Michtoms continued to produce bears on an as needed basis until their ability to meet the demand soon outstripped their production capabilities, and the Ideal company was formed. Ideal did not use permanent labels in the beginning but by studying known examples you can soon learn to distinguish them. In 1982 CBS took over the company and Teddy Bears ceased to be a part of the program.

AETNA

In business for a short span of perhaps two years, ca. 1906, this trade stamped their name on the foot pad. This logo often faded, but close examination can reveal traces.

BRUIN MANUFACTURING CO.

This is another firm that enjoyed success for a brief time during the same era as Aetna. A black ribbon stamped B M C in gold was sewn across the foot pad.

COLUMBIA MANUFACTURING CO.

The Columbia Manufacturing Company was also in business pre-1910. The only teddy from this works that can positively be identified is the "laughing Roosevelt bear."

APPLAUSE

Applause began in 1981, primarily making toys for children. For the past several years they have produced and distributed Robert Raikes designs.

GUND

Gund is a relatively long-lived company that began in 1898. They say teddy production began before 1910, but I know of no bears from that time. 1930s to 1950s bears are mostly made of plush and are unjointed. In 1964 they obtained the right to make Winnie The Pooh characters and still hold the license to do so. Most products are labeled and therefore easy to identify. They continue to supply an affordable line of Poohs and other bears for mass marketing.

KNICKERBOCKER

An old company which began in 1850, Knickerbocker introduced their first teddy around 1920. Over the years the firm has experienced reverses by being sold, undergoing bankruptcy and has been resurrected by new owners. Ironically the present proprietors have the surname of Knickerbocker. A good many of their earlier products can be found with labels intact.

American companies no longer in business are Strauss, Character, and California Stuffed Toys. Still in operation are Commonwealth, Dakin, Eden, Russ Berrie, and North American Bears.

GREAT BRITAIN

J. K. FARNELL

The first Farnell bear was introduced in 1908, and its most distinctive characteristic is five joined claws embroidered on the paw pad. Farnell is renowned for having made the original "Pooh" belonging to Christopher Robin Milne. They ceased doing business in 1968, but in the 1990s the Merrythought firm registered the Farnell name and are therefore able to use the name on selected products.

DEAN'S RAG BOOK

Dean's began doing business in London in 1903. They are now located in Wales and use the name "Dean's Childplay Toys Ltd." The majority of their labeling remains, since in most cases the label was sewn on all four sides.

MERRYTHOUGHT

Merrythought has also used joined claws on the paw pad, but there are four and not five as are found on Farnell's work. Their methods of labeling have been celluloid buttons, foot labels, and hang tags. This has been a family owned enterprise since 1919 and still holds an illustrious position in the marketplace.

CHILTERN

Chiltern began in 1924 and was ultimately acquired by Chad Valley in 1967.

The Chiltern label was sewn on and read Chiltern Hygienic Toys. After the firm was acquired by Chad Valley the tag read Chiltern/Chad Valley.

CHAD VALLEY

Chad Valley introduced their first teddy in 1920. Their methods of marking bears has been to use a celluloid button, followed by an aerolite button and cloth labels. In 1938 they received the Royal Warrant, and from that time on the labels have so stated.

CANTERBURY

Maude and John Blackburn named their family run business after the town where they are located.

They have been making their distinctive teddies since 1980.

LITTLE FOLK

Most of their bears are unjointed but imaginatively dressed. In operation since 1976, they use a brass medal hung from a brass chain around the teddy's neck.

PEDIGREE

This company had locations in both England and Ireland and that is so stated on the sewn-in tag. They went out of business in 1988.

GABRIELLE DESIGNS LTD.

Gabrielle is located in Yorkshire and has been a vital and respected part of the bear community. The business was founded in 1968 by Shirley Clarkson as a cottage industry conducted from her home. A year later her husband joined the firm to assist in marketing and finance. In 1972 Shirley designed the first Paddington Bear and was granted a license to make and sell the product worldwide by Michael Bond, author of the Paddington books. At that time only the 20 inch bear was manufactured and was so successful all other designs were discontinued.

Gabrielle Designs factory and a group of bear enthusiasts.

23

Until 1985 the company produced no products other than Paddington, but sales declined during the next three years. Other designs were then introduced including Scottish and toweling bears and in 1992 a license to produce and sell a line of Pooh and his friends was granted by the Walt Disney Company. Paddington, Aunt Lucy, and three sets of Pooh have been issued in limited editions in attractive designs and presentations.

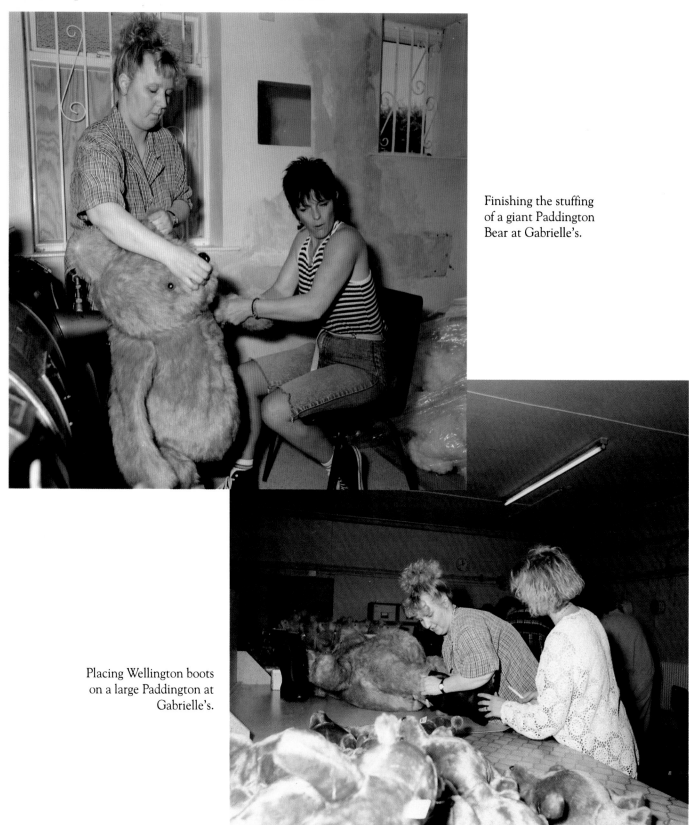

Finishing the stuffing of a giant Paddington Bear at Gabrielle's.

Placing Wellington boots on a large Paddington at Gabrielle's.

In 1994 the company was reorganized under new management with Stephen Beaumont joining the firm as a consultant for business development. Mr. Beaumont then led the management team, in an agreement with Clarkson, to acquire the total shareholding. As managing director, Mr. Beaumont is currently taking the firm in a new direction by introducing more classic designs meant for the adult collector. Among his goals is the intent to employ well known artists to design limited editions under the Gabrielle label.

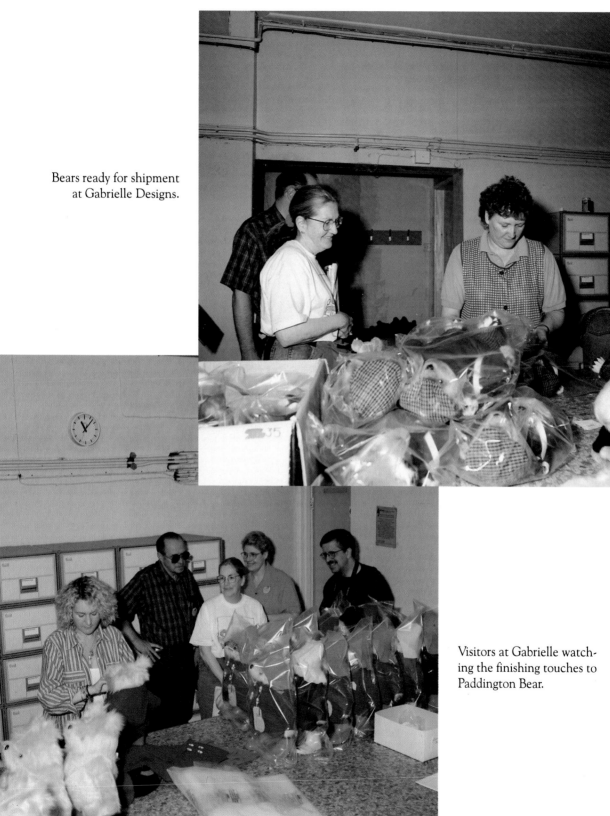

Bears ready for shipment at Gabrielle Designs.

Visitors at Gabrielle watching the finishing touches to Paddington Bear.

Margaret Strong, collector extraordinaire, the museum houses the finest assemblage of dolls, but also places great emphasis on teddies. For its grand opening a special Steiff teddy was made and Hans Otto Steiff, now deceased, was present for signing these delectable creations. Over the years many other bears have been created by Steiff under the Strong name and have been available in the museum's gift shop. For the past several years, the museum, in conjunction with the Steiff Company, has hosted a bear affair. Scores of attendees participate in the lectures offered and in the many family oriented activities. A show and sale with well known dealers selling new and old bears is a main attraction. Steiff representatives are present along with fabulous toys from their archives in Germany. This a rare opportunity to see playthings not normally available for viewing.

Left: The show and sale attendees at the Strong Museum.

Below: Susannah Steiff Pinyuh (Richard's grand-daughter) signing bears at the Strong Museum.

Bottom Left: A *Dicky* bear from the Steiff archives on display at the Strong Museum.

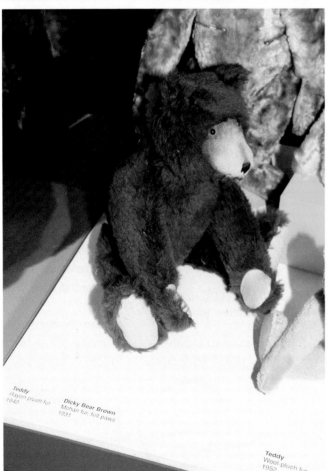

Teddy
Rayon plush fur
1940

Dicky Bear Brown
Mohair fur, felt paws
1931

Teddy
Wool-plush fur
1952

Archival wonders are also showcased at the Steiff Festival held each year in Toledo, Ohio, under the sponsorship of the Toy Store. This is a convention that has been held for 10 years to date and is always much anticipated.

Steiff has a lovely museum within their factory complex in Giengen, Germany. The story of the company's beginning and its subsequent growth is unfolded along with a display of their marvelous products over the years. This destination is high on the

Jörg Junginger (great-grandson of Margarete Steiff) at Steiff Festival IX in 1994.

Steiff Museum display window featuring Richard Steiff's portrait, bust of Theodore Roosevelt and pre-1935 teddies.

Steiff Museum display window.

list of arctophiles everywhere and is a not-to-be forgotten experience. There are other museums worth visiting while in Germany. Nürnberg was the acknowledged toy capital of the world pre-World War II and the city teemed with establishments in the bear making business. While the most famous were

Nürnberg Museum Poster.

Bing and Schuco, lesser known firms and cottage industries were in full force. The Spielzeugmuseum (Toy Museum) has a superlative collection that I highly recommend. Along with beer halls and oop-pa-pa, Munich also has a toy museum with many teddies arranged in charming ways. It is a rather small building with a lighthouse-type staircase, but it has a delightful collection and should not be overlooked.

Teddies at the Munich Museum

The Toy Museum in Munich.

On December 5, 1994, in South Kensington, London, Christie's held an auction which had extraordinary results. Lot number 32 was a circa 1904 Steiff teddy that had been the companion of Colonel T. R. Henderson who was a force in the U.K. branch of Good Bears Of The World. The final hammer price of £110,000, or approximately $171,600, set a record not soon to be topped. The proud new owner Mr. Sekiguchi planned to showcase *Teddy Girl* in his new museum in Izu, Japan.

Leyla Maniera, auctioneer and Teddy Bear specialist at Christie's in London, holding *Teddy Girl* in December 1994 when the bear was sold. *Courtesy of Christie's London.*

The Izu Museum opened in 1995 to record crowds and continues to attract visitors the world over. From the moment the huge animated, talking bear welcomes you at the door you know an unusual treat is in store. Along with *Teddy Girl* there are sizable panoplies of recognizable stage, literature, and screen works. They include *A Christmas Carol, Gone With The Wind, The Nutcracker* and my two favorites, *The Sound Of Music* and *E. T.* They sing, they sway, they dance, and *E.T.'s* finger lights up. What imagination! It's like a bear Disneyland.

The Izu Museum, Japan.

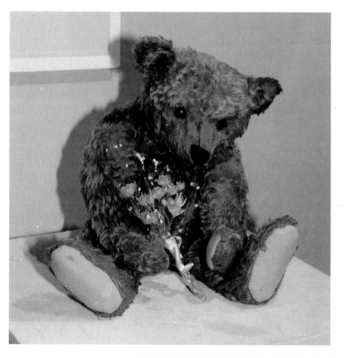

Above: Teddy Girl at her new home at the Izu Museum.

American and Canadians who visited the Izu Museum in 1994 and the owner Mr. Sekiguchi.

Garden statuary at the Izu Museum.

Hanky available in the gift shop at the Izu Museum.

"E. T." at the Izu Museum.

The biggest museum devoted entirely to teddies is in Naples, Florida. Housed in an attractive woodland setting, the museum features over 2,300 bears. There are audio-visual displays to visit and bruins from antique examples to limited editions are showcased, as well as those in art, sculpture, and every other media imaginable. It is a veritable wonderland stemming from one woman's collection. A trip to Florida would not be complete without entering this glorious return to a childhood fantasy.

Sign at the Naples, Florida Museum.

Parade of Teddies at the Naples Museum.

The Courtyard at the Naples Museum.

Carved bears at the Naples Museum.

There are several places in England where one can immerse oneself in teddies. For *Rupert* fans there is a museum dedicated solely to him in Canterbury. Other enjoyments can be found at Bethnal Green and Pollock's in London; The Toy And Teddy Bear museum in St. Anne's, Lancashire; and The Museum of Childhood in Edinburgh.

There are many shops all over the globe that house a mini-museum because the owners themselves are collectors. One of the first mini-museums to open was in Doris and Terry Michaud's beautiful Victorian shop in Chesaning, Michigan.

Margaret and Gerry Grey's shop in Northhampton.

Mutan House, operated by Mr. Gawase in Tokyo, also has a growing collection.

A special treat can be found at two, and probably more, lovely locations in England. Margaret and Gerry Grey's shop in Wellingborough, Northhampton, is located in a listed building of historical merit. Besides being shop owners and collectors, the Greys are deeply involved in other aspects of the bear world. They continually showcase and sponsor artists and they hosted the 1993 convention "Teddies Of The World." Future events are planned and eagerly anticipated, for the fellowship enjoyed is one of the pluses in the Teddy Bear Universe.

The sign outside the Grey's historical shop.

Margaret and Gerry Grey inside their shop.

A group of old bears displayed in the Inglenook fireplace in the Grey's shop.

A collection of one-of-a-kind and special artist bears that the Grey's sell and promote.

The Grey's grandson among the shop's bears.

Ian Pout's shop, Teddy Bears of Witney, is on the opposite side of England in Oxfordshire. The shop and museum are special because Ian is the owner of Alfonzo the Steiff bear that is red and is dressed as a Cossack. Alfonzo has a Russian provenance, having once belonged to Princess Xenia, a relative of the ill fated Romanovs. Mr. Pout commissioned Steiff to produce a replica of Alfonzo in 1990. That limited edition has sold out and there is now a smaller version that is also proving to be popular.

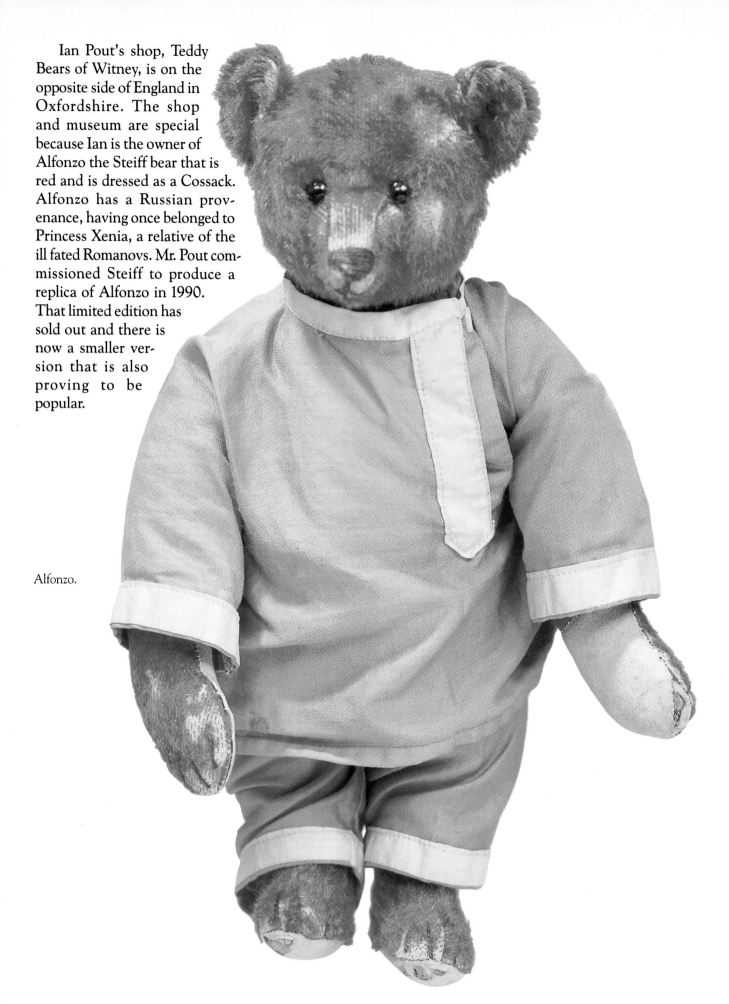

Alfonzo.

"The Teddy Bears of Witney" in Oxfordshire owned by Ian Pout.

Ian Pout holding the famous *Alfonzo*.

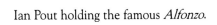

Alfonzo in his special cabinet on display in the mini-museum.

The attractive Witney shop and valued employees.

A perfect example of Steiff's 1912 black bear; named "Othello" by his owner Ian Pout.

An unusual ca. 1953 teddy displayed in the museum at Witney.

Ca. 1940 Japanese bears on display at Witney.

United Kingdom artist bears.

43

The ultimate bear experience can be found in Berne, Switzerland, whose very name means "bear." Bear flags fly above the colonnaded passages, bear statues of every description grace the squares and crowds quickly gather when the chimes announce the regalia of the mechanical bear clock that has thrilled people for hundreds of years. Most famous in Berne are the bear pits where, for centuries, these charming creatures have amused visitors.

Teddy Bear shows and conventions have become a way of life for the bear aficionado and show no sign of abating. They are held all over the world on a regular basis and the beginning collector will find much to study and compare before getting their feet wet. There are teddies and realistic bears to suit every taste whether one wants to become owners or just observe their proud majesty.

The mechanical bear clock in Berne, Switzerland.

Bear statue in Berne.

How about a treat?

The Bear Pit at Berne.

Children at play; Bear Pit at Berne.

44

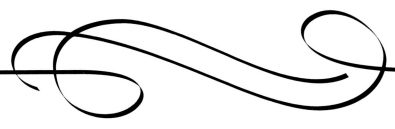

Chapter III
Snips And Snails

What are Teddy Bears made of? Well, not quite what little boys are made of, but there are enough components to confuse the novice until he or she becomes familiar with the terminology. The Glossary which follows will help sort things out.

American Bear: 30" ca. 1908; tan mohair; replaced eyes; original leather pads; signed on one foot pad "Sylvia Clegg, Calumet, Michigan 1903"; (probably her birth); the writing has been authenticated; $4,000-$4,500.

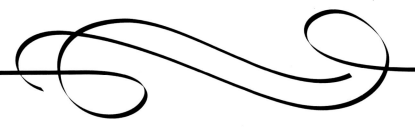

Glossary

Celluloid: A synthetic material that resembles plastic; often used for logo buttons.

Center seam: Refers to a seam on a teddy's head running down the center of the face. This process allowed the economical utilization of all the mohair on a bolt.

Chest tag: A paper, metal or plastic logo attached to the bear's chest.

Clipped mohair: Fur that is clipped short on specific areas; frequently the muzzle.

Cloth nose: A fabric, often rep, that is generally triangular in shape and stitched in place on the nose area; found primarily on American bears.

Dralon: A synthetic fabric that was developed in the 1950s and was used in place of mohair.

Excelsior: Shaved wood filings used as filling

Hang tag: A paper tag hung around the bear's neck and containing all pertinent information.

Hump: Found on bears until sometime after W. W. II, the hump on the back emulated the feature found on some living bruins.

Inset muzzle: Extra pattern pieces that are seamed into the face.

Kapok: Soft filling material that comes from trees and is used often in British-made bears.

Limited edition: Bears made only in a certain number.

Mohair: A natural fiber garnered from the angora goat; principal material used in bear making.

Plush: A synthetic fabric used generally in less expensive bears or when it is more appropriate to the design; it *can* be unique and as costly as mohair.

Replica: An edition of bears using an old pattern to reproduce a vintage product.

Rexine: A coated canvas used for paw pads; it often flaked off.

Rod bear: Refers to the method of articulating the first teddies made by Steiff; metal rods run from the head to the end of the body and there joined other rods to enable limbs to move; can be determined by X-raying.

Sealing wax: Material used for molding the nose on a rod bear.

Shoe button eyes: Made of leather covered wood and used in all sizes for teddy bear eyes.

Tipped mohair: Mohair that is one color and dyed another hue on the ends.

Yes/No: A method used by Schuco that has inner metal workings; by levering the tail the head moves both vertically and horizontally.

In America the use of mohair was prevalent until the mid 1930s when plush came into vogue and was used on less expensive bears. At this time pink and blue colors began to appear on bears as well. Excelsior was the preferred stuffing, followed by cotton. Both fillings were used intermittently. Shoe button eyes were initially used, but as early as 1907 glass eyes were often substituted. For the most part noses, mouths, and claws were embroidered, but many American products possessed cloth noses that were sewn on. Pads were made primarily of felt.

In Germany, bears were consistently made of mohair except for periods during both world wars when other fabrics were more available. Excelsior and even floor scraps can be detected as stuffing during bear surgery. As in American bears, both shoe button and glass eyes allowed German teddies to see. Felt pads, lined in both cardboard and another layer of any colored felt, were used for strength on larger sizes. Noses, mouths, and claws were embroidered in black or brown, except on white bears where a rosy tan was used.

Great Britain is, as far as I know, the only country to use rexine for paw pads. This is a useful tool to determine country of origin in the absence of tags. English mohair is especially silky and its use superseded other fabrics most of the time. The employment of two stuffing materials was also prevalent; generally excelsior in the head and kapok in the body. Shoe button and glass eyes, felt pads and embroidered features were used in approximately the same proportion as the use in other countries.

When reading descriptions of bears in the text assume the bears will have all of these components and also be jointed, unless otherwise stated.

Another snip of information deals with the issue of provenance. Some collectors are avid to learn about their bear's history. In most cases this is not possible, since during the passage of time the teddy has usually changed hands several times, and all data has been lost. On occasion a teddy will be offered for sale by the owner or the owner's descendants. In that case information can be documented and is known as the provenance.

The question arises as to what added value, if any, a provenance places on the bear. In general not much; it only serves as a bit of lore that is rather dear to the heart and one can indulge in a bit of romancing. Of course in some cases the bear may have belonged to such a famous or heroic figure that the price can explode and even then *that* figure is determined by the buyer and how much the ownership of such a bear means to him or her. When the teddy is accompanied by letters and photographs this will jockey the price even higher, and rightly so. Occasionally a bear will appear on the market or at auction that was previously owned by an ordinary, everyday person. The attending data can be so sweet or so filled with pathos that one yearns to possess it. In that instance one can pay more than the bear's actual dollar value. Is that a mistake? Well, no, as a collector I occasionally fall into that buyer mentality myself. You must remember that if you make such a purchase and the time for selling arises, the next buyer may not be as charmed as you were. Basically the best criteria for assembling a collection of teddies is to buy what you love and want to live with and not what the bear may be worth in the future. I wish you a joyful collecting experience.

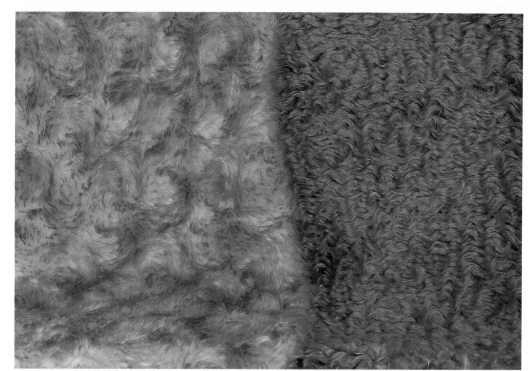

Tipped and solid color mohair.

Teddy Bear Purse: 6.50" seated; 16" overall; this large handbag is pictured with a photograph of the owner holding it; ca. 1918. Made of mohair; lined in rexine and with shoe button eyes, it is fully jointed. *Photo Courtesy of Christie's, London.*

Steevans Bear: 9.50"; the previous owner of this teddy named *Pery* was William Pery Goodbody 1905-1942. He was educated at Shrewsbury and Cambridge and rowed for both. Each year at Henley-On-Thames there is a regatta, and this teddy is special because he is wearing his owner's medals. *Pery* is gold mohair and has shoe button eyes. Ca. 1918 he retains his logo button inscribed *Steevans England PT 126846* in his ear. *Photo Courtesy of Christie's, London.*

Steiff Bear *Theodore*: 3.50"; this gold mohair teddy with black bead eyes was given to the British actor Peter Bull (shown in photograph) in 1948 to celebrate an opening night. For 35 years the two were inseparable, for Peter carried the tiny bear in his pocket. At age 16 Peter had suffered a trauma for, while at boarding school, his Mother had disposed of his childhood Teddy Bear. Many years later he admitted this at a dinner party and discovered he wasn't alone in his teddy experience. The stories related by others were ultimately published in book form and Peter became a cause celebre on national television. A grown man declaring his love for Teddies influenced those who secretly felt the same way to finally admit it. The bear hunt was on. Teddy Bears appeared at his door constantly and one of these teddies became as famous as Peter himself. The bear was of course, the appealing creature who played the role of "Aloysius" in the television drama *Brideshead Revisited.* Peter Bull was a charming and witty man who was mourned at his death by all who ever knew him either personally or by his tremendous influence in the world of bears. *Photo Courtesy of Christie's, London.*

Merrythought *Mr. Whoppit:* 9"; this unique bear of cream mohair, glass eyes and dressed in a felt jacket is ca. 1956. His provenance is both exciting and heart wrenching for he was the mascot of the super speed hero Donald Campbell. When "Mr. Whoppit" was sold in December of 1995, along with an immense amount of Campbell archival material, Christie's catalogue described him as follows: "Donald Campbell was a compulsive record-breaker on land and water in the 1950s and 1960s. His cars and boats were all called *Bluebird.* Whenever Campbell tried for a record, his mascot *Mr. Whoppit* went with him. Together they broke the water speed record seven times, reaching 276 mph in 1964. In that year they also broke the land speed record in Australia with 403.1 mph. They survived several spectacular crashes, but Campbell's luck ran out on January 4, 1967. On Coniston Water in England, a new record was in sight with an outward run of 290 mph. But tragedy struck on the return run when *Bluebird's* nose lifted and with Campbell and *Mr. Whoppit* she then plunged into the depths at 300 mph. "She's tramping...the water's not good...I can't see much...I'm going...I'm on my back...I've gone." With those words over the radio, Donald Campbell's life came to an end." Campbell's body was never found, but *Mr. Whoppit* floated to the surface and ultimately became Campbell's daughter's companion in *her* racing career. *Courtesy of Christie's, London.*

German Bear: 14"; *Uncle Edward* belonged to Miss Alfreda Alice Annie Elderfield (1907-1994) of London. The bear was given to Alfreda on her first birthday and became a constant companion. The imaginative child devised games and even a family for her friend. *Uncle Edward* was such an integral part of the household that some of the postcards shown are addressed to him. The 4" teddy, also pictured, is his toy. *Uncle Edward* is made of white mohair and has shoe button eyes. Though worn, his lovable face and provenance, including photos of Alfreda, would make him a warm addition to any collection.
Photo Courtesy of Christie's, London.

CHAPTER IV
THE BEARS AT HOME

Welcome. Come into our house and out to our garden and woods.

American Bear: 18" ca. 1907; cinnamon mohair; glass eyes; cloth nose; no ID; $950-$1,000. *Alice Channing Collection.*

American Bear: 15" ca. 1910; gold mohair; shoe button eyes; cloth nose; excelsior and cotton stuffed; no ID; $950-$1,050. *Alice Channing Collection.*

Artist Bear: 13.50" ca. 1990; made by Barbara Sixby; $295-$325. *Alice Channing Collection.*

Steiff Bears: 30", 30" and 24" ca. 1910 (largest) and 1925. All described elsewhere.

Steiff Bear: 16" ca. 1910; tan mohair; shoe button eyes; original muzzle and leash; printed button; $6,000-$6,500.

Steiff Bear: 19" 1912; for the English market only; black sealskin type mohair (1214 only in this fabric); shoe button eyes backed by red felt; no ID; price is what the market will bear (black Steiff bears have realized from $20,000 to $45,000 at auction.)

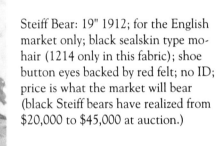

Steiff Bear: 16" ca. 1910; tan mohair; shoe button eyes; no ID; dress not original; $1,500-$1,600.

English Farnell Bear; 17" ca. 1955; gold mohair; glass eyes; no ID; $800-$900.

Steiff Bear: 20" 1991; black curly mohair; Ltd. ed. of 3,000 for the British market; presentation box. $500-$550.

Steiff Bear: 20" ca. 1907; tan mohair; center head seam; shoe button eyes; printed button; $5,000-$6,000.

Steiff Bear: 24" 1926; cream mohair with brown tipping (faded); oversize glass eyes; $6,500-$7,500.

Steiff Bear: 12" ca. 1912; white mohair; glass eyes; flannel pads; printed button; $1,700-$1,800.

Opposite page: Steiff Bear: 3.50" ca. 1910; tan mohair; black bead eyes; printed button; $850-$950.

Steiff Bear: 20" ca. 1910; off white mohair; shoe button eyes; printed button; $3,400-$3,500.

Steiff Bear:14" ca. 1910; pale cinnamon mohair; shoe button eyes; printed button; $1,500-$1,600.

Steiff Bear: 14" described above.

Steiff Bear: 9.50" ca. 1910; pale cinnamon mohair; shoe button eyes; printed button; $1,150-$1,250.

Steiff Bear: 24" ca. 1925; white mohair; glass eyes; printed button; $4,500-$5,500.

Opposite page:

Top Left: Steiff Bear: 10" ca. 1909; tan mohair; shoe button eyes; no ID; $1,100-$1,200.

Top Right: English Farnell Bear: 19" ca. 1930; pale gold mohair; glass eyes; no ID; $1,600-$1,700.

Bottom Left: Steiff Bear: 12" ca. 1960; caramel mohair; glass eyes; dressed by F A O Schwarz; $500-$550.

Bottom Right: Steiff *Jackie* Bear: 14" 1953; blonde mohair; glass eyes; stitch across nose; airbrushed belly button; Jubilee bear; raised script button; $1,200-$1,400.

Right: Artist Marching Bears: 12" and 17". Designed and made by author in 1985; $650 set.

Below: Steiff Record Teddy: 10" ca. 1914; white mohair; shoe button eyes; on metal cart with wooden wheels that presents a pumping action when pulled; printed button; $3,500-$3,800.

Bottom Right: Steiff Studio Bear: 36" 1970s and 1980s; tan mohair; plastic eyes; brass button and red studio tag; $1,100-$1,200.

English Farnell Bear: 21" ca. 1926; blonde mohair; glass eyes; no
ID; $1,900-$2,100.

Steiff Bear: 30" ca. 1950; rosy tan mohair; glass eyes; raised script button; $2,500-$2,900 (small bear described on page 60.)

American Bear: 12.50" ca. 1907; gold mohair; glass eyes; made by Bruin; no ID; $1,500-$1,600. Steiff Bear: 15" ca. 1904; cinnamon mohair; shoe button eyes; no ID; $3,500-$4,000.

American Bear: 12.50" ca. 1908; tan mohair; shoe button eyes; no ID; hat and beads not original; $700-$800.

Beaver Valley *Tucker*: 18" 1987; plush; hand made eyes and hinged mouth with teeth; original clothes; hang tag and foot signature; $500-$550.

Steiff Bear: 30" ca. 1907; apricot mohair; shoe button eyes; cone shaped nose; no ID; $9,000-$9,500.

Beaver Valley Polar Bear: 26"
1990; white plush; hand made
eyes and hinged jaw with
teeth; ltd. ed. of 25; signed on
foot; $900-$1,000.

Schuco Yes/No Bear: 17" ca. 1925; cream mohair with lavender tipping; glass eyes; folded paper tag; $4,500-$5,000.
American Ideal Bear: 12" ca. 1908; gold mohair; shoe button eyes; no ID; $800-$900.

American Bear: 16" ca. 1907; gold mohair; shoe button eyes; no ID; $1,400-$1,500.

Steiff Bear: 20" ca. 1905; white
mohair that has silvered; shoe button eyes; center head seam; no ID;
$6,500-$7,000.

Steiff Bears: 24" and 20"; both bears described on pages 61 and above.

CHAPTER V
UP CLOSE AND PERSONAL

Chad Valley *Sooty* Bear: 15" ca. 1950; gold mohair; black ears; *Harry Corbet*, television puppeteer, performed with a puppet he named *Sooty*. It was replicated in both hand puppets and teddies by Chad Valley; tag under arm; $185-$195; *Susan Stanton-Reid Collection.*

Steiff *Dicky* Bear: 13" ca. 1930; gold mohair; glass eyes; replaced pads; (this and the wear brings the price down); printed button; $1,400-$1,600.

Steiff Replica *Dicky* Bear showing how the original mouth was airbrushed smiling.

Steiff Replica *Dicky* Bear showing how the original version had airbrushed velvet pads.

Steiff *Petsy* Bear: 24" ca. 1925; cream mohair tipped reddish brown; head seam bisects between the ears and runs down the muzzle to the nose; blue eyes; rosy red mouth, nose, and claws; oversized wired ears; replica chest tag; $11,000-$13,000.

Steiff Bear: 13" ca. 1930; pink mohair that has been renewed to the original color; glass eyes; printed button; $1,200-$1,400 (note that a perfect Teddy Rose in original color and untouched would be several thousand dollars more).

English Farnell Bear: 28" ca. 1935; gold mohair; glass eyes; no ID; $1,800-$2,000.

German Bear: 24" ca. 1950; cream and brown tipped mohair; glass eyes; open mouth with felt tongue; no ID; possibly made by Anker. $350-$400. *Susan Stanton-Reid Collection.*

English Merrythought *Cheeky* Bear: 26" ca. 1975; gold mohair; velvet muzzle; plastic eyes; tag on foot; $700-$800.

Artist Bear: 14" 1992; made by author for Disney Convention in Anaheim, California; ltd. edition of 25; $350.

Artist Bear; 25"; made for the 1992 Convention at Disneyland by Jeanette Warner; one of a kind; sold for $1,150.

Schuco Yes/No Bear: 17" ca. 1948; tan mohair; glass eyes; molded
nose; music box that winds from the front; no ID; $2,300-$2,500.

CHAPTER VI
HOLD THAT POSE

American Bear: 12" ca 1907; reddish gold mohair;
shoe button eyes; attributed to Ideal; no ID;
$1,300-$1,500. *Ken Yenke Collection.*

Steiff Bear: 12" ca. 1905; blonde mohair; shoe button eyes; blank button; $1,800-$2,000. *Alice Channing Collection.*

Steiff Bear On Cast Wheels: 22" ca. 1907; off-white mohair; swivel head; shoe button eyes; blank button; $2,500-$3,000.
Steiff Muzzle Bear: 16" ca. 1910; tan mohair; original muzzle and leash; printed button; $6,500-$7,000.

American Bear: 28" ca. 1907; gold mohair; shoe button eyes; probably made by Aetna; no ID; $3,500-$3,700.

American Bear: 18" ca. 1906; brown coat wool; shoe button eyes; linen pads; red painted wooden mouth and white teeth; appears to be made by Columbia Teddy Bear Company; no ID; $2,500-$3,000.

Steiff Bear: 20" ca. 1907; white mohair; shoe button eyes; the sailor suit was made especially for this bear but was not originally issued with it; sold at *Christie's* auction in 1995 for approximately $20,000. *Courtesy of Christie's, London.*

German Bear: 17" ca. 1919; gold mohair; shoe button eyes; replaced pads (long ago with leather); possibly a Bing; $1,000-$1,100. *Gail Norris Collection.*

Steiff Bear: 9" ca. 1910; mohair; shoe button eyes; purported to have been produced for a U. S. Dept. Store; some of the clothes are very old and some are not; owner called it "The Traveling Bear." Printed button. $1,800 complete. *Susan Stanton-Reid Collection.*

Left: American Bear: 15" ca. 1915; short bristly gold mohair; glass eyes; stick figure construction; clothes not original; no ID; $325-$350. *Gail Norris Collection.*

Right: English Farnell Bear: 22" ca. 1918; blond mohair; glass eyes; joined paw claws; no ID; $2,200-$2,500.

German Clown Bear: 10" ca. 1920; wool head; felt clown outfit forms the body; swivel head; pin jointed arms; no ID; $125-$150. *Susan Stanton-Reid Collection.*

American Bears: 24" and 22" ca. 1915; gold mohair; glass eyes; fabric noses; smaller bear has replaced ears; no ID; $400+ each. *Susan Stanton-Reid Collection.*

American Bear: 21" ca. 1920; gold mohair; glass eyes; no ID; $600-$650. *Alice Channing Collection.*

Teddy Bear Purse: 9.50" ca. 1920; gold mohair; shoe button eyes; body forms rexine lined handbag; no ID; sold at *Christie's* auction in 1994 for approximately $1,100. *Courtesy of Christie's, London.*

Schuco Bears: 3.50" and 5" ca. 1925; green perfume; tan bear has a flexible body center that pushes down (unusual—possibly a squeaker at one time); tan compact bear; no ID; $450+ each.

Schuco Yes/No Bear: 20"
1930s; lavender tipped mohair; glass eyes; no ID;
$4,000+. *Courtesy of David
Douglass.*

English Peacock Bear: 28" ca. 1930; gold mohair; glass eyes;
felt pads; jacket not original; label on foot; $2,000-$2,200.

German Musical Helvetic Bear: 16" ca. 1930; white mohair; glass eyes; original hat and ruff; since Helvetia is the
Latin name for Switzerland, it is assumed the squeeze music box came from that country; $1,800-$2,000. *Ken
Yenke Collection.*

American Bear: 24" ca. 1930; brown mohair; glass eyes; excelsior and cotton stuffed; made by Knickerbocker; no ID; $750-$800.

German Jopi *Jackie* Bear: 18" 1934; pale gold mohair; glass eyes; identified from 1934 Jopi catalog; $3,000+. *Courtesy of David Douglass.*

Schuco Yes/No Bear: 20" 1930s; gold mohair; glass eyes; no ID; $2,000+. *Courtesy of David Douglass.*

Schuco Yes/No Bear: 9" ca. 1930; gold wool plush; tri-colored side-glancing glass eyes; velvet pads; no ID; $1,400-$1,500.

German Jopi Bellows Music Box Bear: 28" 1930s; mohair; glass eyes; no ID; $8,000+. *Courtesy of David Douglass.*

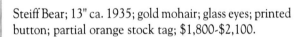

Steiff Bear; 13" ca. 1935; gold mohair; glass eyes; printed button; partial orange stock tag; $1,800-$2,100.

German Crämer Bear: 14" 1930s; gold mohair; glass eyes; no ID; $1,800+. *Courtesy of David Douglass.*

English Merrythought Bear: 19" ca. 1930; gold mohair; glass eyes; joined paw claws; celluloid button in right ear; label on foot; paper hang tag; $1,600-$1,700.

English Baby Bear: 10" ca. 1935; made by Chad Valley; brown alpaca; glass eyes; swivel head and arms; celluloid button; Manchester Dept. Store label; $725-$800.

Above: English Bear: 30" ca. 1935; faded blue cotton plush; glass eyes; no ID; $300-$325.
English Chiltern Bear; 17" ca. 1935; gold mohair and faded blue plush; glass eyes; unjointed; Dutch style teddy; no ID; $450-$475. *Susan Stanton-Reid Collection.*

Above Right: German Crämer Bear: 20" 1930s; Blond mohair; glass eyes; open mouth; no ID; $3,500+. *Courtesy of David Douglass.*

Right: Knickerbocker Bears: 13", 16", and 20" ca. 1930 and 1940; gold mohair; velvet pads; inset muzzles; glass eyes on largest and smallest bears; celluloid roll around eyes on middle size; label on smallest; $125-$450. *Susan Stanton-Reid Collection.*

Opposite Page: Knickerbocker Bear: 12" ca. 1935; gold mohair; inset muzzle; velvet pads; painted metal eyes; no ID; $250-$275. *Susan Stanton-Reid Collection.*

English *Ivy* and *Brumus* Polar Bears: 19"; made by Dean's to celebrate the birth of a cub at the London Zoo in 1949; label; hang tag; $1,100-$1,200.

Knickerbocker Bears: 12.50", 13", 14", 16" ca. 1940 to 1950; small bear is unjointed plush with plastic eyes; the rest are mohair with inset muzzles and velvet pads; the two brown bears have glass eyes; and the cinnamon has eyes of painted metal; labels sewn into side seams; $35 for plush bear; $350-$450 for mohair. *Susan Stanton-Reid Collection.*

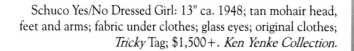

Schuco Yes/No Dressed Girl: 13" ca. 1948; tan mohair head, feet and arms; fabric under clothes; glass eyes; original clothes; *Tricky* Tag; $1,500+. *Ken Yenke Collection.*

English Chiltern Bear: 15" ca. 1930; gold mohair; glass eyes; velvet pads; no ID; $1,100-$1,200.

Irish Bear: 15" ca. 1940; white mohair; glass eyes; rexine pads; leather covered wooden mouth that can be opened or closed by pressing together two amber balls at the back of the head; made by Tara; no ID; $800-$900.

German Crämer *Bearkins*: 11" 1930s; mohair; glass eyes; felt mouths; dressed and accessorized by F A O Schwarz; $1,500+ each. *Courtesy of David Douglass.*

Steiff Bear: 29" ca. 1950; curly rosy tan mohair; glass eyes; no ID; $2,600-$2,700.

American Bear: 13" ca. 1950; mohair; plastic eyes; velvet muzzle; felt pads; bells sewn on front; partial tag in front seam; made by Knickerbocker; $250-$300.

Austrian Bear: 16" ca. 1950; plush head and paws; made-on clothes featuring embroidered cotton shirt and the balance of felt; non-jointed; glass eyes; no ID; $50-$60.
English Pedigree Bear: 17" ca. 1950; gold mohair; glass eyes; felt nose; velvet pads; tie, umbrella and hat not original; $250-$300. *Susan Stanton-Reid Collection.*

English Chiltern Bear: 15" ca. 1930; gold mohair; glass eyes; velvet pads; no ID; $1,100-$1,200.

Irish Bear: 15" ca. 1940; white mohair; glass eyes; rexine pads; leather covered wooden mouth that can be opened or closed by pressing together two amber balls at the back of the head; made by Tara; no ID; $800-$900.

German Crämer *Bearkins*: 11" 1930s; mohair; glass eyes; felt mouths; dressed and accessorized by F A O Schwarz; $1,500+ each. *Courtesy of David Douglass.*

English Chiltern *Home Guard* Bear: 12.50" ca. 1940; mohair; glass eyes; made-on velvet uniform; felt hat; unusual and rarely found; no ID; $400-$500. *Ian Pout Collection.*

Knickerbocker Bear: 10" ca. 1950; mohair; glass eyes; unjointed; no ID; $75. Knickerbocker Bear: 14" ca. 1950; plush; plastic eyes; inset muzzle; label; $125-$150. *Susan Stanton-Reid Collection.*

Steiff Bear Doll: 9" ca. 1945; rayon plush head and paws; rayon body and limbs; glass eyes; printed button; $1,450-$1,500.

Schuco Yes/No Bear: 16" 1948; tan mohair; glass eyes; molded nose; key wound music box; *Tricky* Tag; $2,300-$2,500.

Steiff Bear: 8" ca. 1950; brown mohair; glass eyes; raised script button; $450-$475.

Steiff Bear: 29" ca. 1950; curly rosy tan mohair; glass eyes; no ID; $2,600-$2,700.

American Bear: 13" ca. 1950; mohair; plastic eyes; velvet muzzle; felt pads; bells sewn on front; partial tag in front seam; made by Knickerbocker; $250-$300.

Austrian Bear: 16" ca. 1950; plush head and paws; made-on clothes featuring embroidered cotton shirt and the balance of felt; non-jointed; glass eyes; no ID; $50-$60.
English Pedigree Bear: 17" ca. 1950; gold mohair; glass eyes; felt nose; velvet pads; tie, umbrella and hat not original; $250-$300. *Susan Stanton-Reid Collection.*

Left: Gebr. Hermann Bear: 15" ca. 1950; gold mohair; glass eyes; no ID; $350-$400.
Gebr. Hermann Bear: 9" ca. 1959; tan mohair; glass eyes; open felt mouth; Teddy-baby type; plastic collar; chest tag; $195-$200. *Susan Stanton-Reid Collection.*

Bottom Left: English Farnell Baby Bear: 10" ca. 1950; mohair; no pads; no ID; $450-$475.

Below: German Bear: 13" ca. 1950; mohair; inset muzzle; open felt mouth; cloth pads; glass eyes; no ID; $225-$245. *Susan Stanton-Reid collection.*

Steiff Bear on Wooden Wheels: 13" ca. 1950; tan mohair; inset muzzle; glass eyes; no ID; $550-$650.

English Twyford Bears: 13", 14", 15" ca. 1950; white, cinnamon, and red mohair; glass eyes (plastic eyes on white); tags sewn into seams; $400-$450 each. *Susan Stanton-Reid Collection.*

English Chad Valley Bear: 27" ca. 1950; tan mohair; glass eyes; typical large nose; label on foot; $1,400-$1,500.

American Bear: 19" ca. 1950; brown alpaca; velvet pads, inner ears and muzzle; glass eyes; excelsior and cotton stuffed; no ID; made by Knickerbocker; $700-$750.

Steiff Zotty Bear: 13.50" ca. 1950; white mohair with apricot chest plate; glass eyes; open felt mouth; raised script button and chest tag; $750-$850. *Ken Yenke Collection.*

Steiff *Teddyli* Bear: 9" ca. 1950; brown mohair head and tops of paws; inset mohair muzzle; open felt mouth; glass eyes; fabric body; cotton shirt; felt jacket and trousers; raised script button; $1,400-$1,500. *Ken Yenke Collection.*

English *Punkinhead:* 16" ca. 1950; Brown and gold mohair with white mohair top of head; velvet inset muzzle; glass eyes; replaced pants; made by Merrythought for Eaton's Dept. Store in Toronto, Canada; sold at *Christie's* London auction in 1994 for approximately $1,575; *Courtesy of Christie's, London.*

Schuco Yes/No Bear: 12" ca. 1950; tan mohair; glass eyes; fur off tail; no ID; $1,200-$1,300.

Schuco Yes/No Bear's tail showing mechanism.

127

Schuco Yes/No Bear: 12" 1953; tan mohair; glass eyes; shows wear; suit not original to bear; no ID; $600-$650.

German Gebr. Hermann Music Bear: 9" ca. 1950; white mohair; glass eyes; open mouth with chain; mounted on musical base; hang tag; $1,500-$1,700. *Ken Yenke Collection.*

Schuco Bear: 19" ca. 1950; gold and brown tipped mohair; inset muzzle; glass eyes; no ID; $650-$750.

Smokey Bear: 17" ca. 1954; plush; vinyl face; glass eyes; blue denim pants; belt with his name; made by Ideal; no ID; $100-$200.

Steiff *Zotty* Bear: 10" ca. 1950; more unusual redwood color tipped mohair; apricot chest plate; glass eyes backed by felt; no ID; $450-$550.

English Chiltern *Ting-A-Ling* Bear; 14" ca. 1953; light gold mohair; glass eyes; rexine pads; bear *chimes* when moved; no ID; $500-$525.

German Petz Bear: 6" ca. 1955; mohair with clipped mohair inset snout, inner ears, paws and feet; googly eyes; Petz button on chest; $500+. *Courtesy of David Douglass.*

English Farnell *Toffee*: 10" ca. 1955; mohair; rexine pads; original knit hat and scarf; based on a character from a radio broadcast; label in back seam; $650-$700.

English *Rupert* Bear; 20" ca. 1958; plush; made-on suit; wears signature checked pants and scarf; made by Burbank Toys; tag on seam; $55-$65.

Steiff Koala Bear: 15" (sitting) ca. 1955; two shades of mohair; glass eyes; felt nose; bent legs; raised script button; $625-$700.

Agnes Brush Pooh: 13" ca. 1955; tan flannel; shoe button eyes; non-jointed; removable cotton knit shirt; no ID; $350+.

German Carnival Bear: 17" ca. 1960; white plush; linen pads; plastic eyes; original bow; no ID; $165-$175.
Schuco Hegi Bear: 11.50" ca. 1960; brown mohair; glass eyes; plastic nose; felt mouth, tongue and pads; original lederhosen (vinyl); non-jointed; no ID; $175-$200. *Susan Stanton-Reid Collection.*

Steiff *Zolac* Bear: 14" ca. 1960; caramel mohair; apricot chest, paws and feet; open felt mouth; glass eyes; raised script button; $550-$600.

English Merrythought *Cheeky* Bear: 13" ca. 1960; tan mohair; glass eyes; velvet muzzle; felt pads; excelsior and kapok stuffed; label on foot; $400-$500.

English Bears and Pandas: 9" to 17" ca. 1960; Unjointed plush; soft filled; plastic eyes; made by Wendy Boston; sewn-on labels; $75+; *Susan Stanton-Reid Collection.*

German Gebr. Hermann Bear: 10" ca. 1960; tan mohair with inset muzzle; glass eyes; no ID; $200-$250.

Steiff *Zooby* Bear: 11" 1964; brown mohair with darker mohair feet; inset muzzle; open felt mouth and claws; plastic eyes; raised script button; $900-$1,000.

Left: English hand knit Bears: 8" to 15" ca. 1960; made during the period that knitting Golliwoggs was also the rage; no ID; $50+; *Susan Stanton-Reid Collection.*

Right: Schuco Bear: 12" ca. 1960; mohair head and arms; made-on soccer clothes; Adidas sneakers; non-jointed bendable; plastic eyes; tagged "Bigo Belo"; $165-$175.

Below: Merrythought *Cheeky* Bears: 12" ca. 1960; gold mohair; velvet inset muzzles; plastic eyes (left) glass eyes (right); labels on feet; $450-$500.

American Gund Pooh: 10" 1964; gold plush; plastic eyes; removable shirt; hat is sewn on; © Disney; label sewn in leg seam; $225-$250.

American Gund Pooh: 23" ca. 1964; gold plush; plastic eyes; yarn nose; © Disney; no ID; $150-$165.

Merrythought's *Mr. and Mrs. Twisty Cheeky*: 11" ca. 1966 gold mohair heads; inset velvet muzzles; plastic eyes; cloth body and paws; felt clothes; labels on feet; sold at *Christie's* in 1995 for approximately $2,850. *Courtesy of Christie's, London.*

English Merrythought Pooh: 26" ca. 1965; gold mohair; plastic eyes; © Disney; tag on foot; $675+.

Steiff *Zotty* Bears: 7" and 10" ca. 1965; frosted mohair; apricot chest plates; plastic eyes; open felt mouth; incised script buttons; $250-$400.

Steiff Studio Bear: 60" as shown in the 1967 catalog; mohair with open mouth; $2,500-$3,000.

Steiff Polar Bears: 16" and 40"; large size is a studio display as shown in the 1967 catalog; $1,500-$1,800.

Steiff Bears: 31.50", 40" and 75.50" the two largest are display bears as shown in the 1967 Steiff catalog; $1,500-$1,800.

Steiff Bears on rubber tired metal wheels; 24" and 18" ca. 1972; brown mohair with inset snout; plastic eyes; incised buttons; $800-$1,000.

German Bear: 20" ca. 1970; curly mohair; open mouth; made by Fechter; tag on ear; $500+.
German Bear: 15" ca. 1980; blond mohair; tan clipped mohair muzzle, inner ears and paw pads; made by Grisly; paper hang tag on chest; $100-$125. *Susan Stanton-Reid Collection.*

Steiff *Papa* Bear: 18" 1980; the first replica made for the collector market; M. I. B. with certificate; $850+.

138

Steiff Prototype: 5" ca. 1980; white *Teddy Baby* never put into production; no ID; $1,750.

Steiff Arm Puppet Bear: 14" 1980; plush; plastic eyes; brass button; split chest tag; $160-$180.

English *Bobby Bear*: 31" ca. 1980; unjointed plush; plastic eyes and nose; wonderfully dressed in wool uniform and hat; leather shoes; made by Alresford Crafts Ltd; tag on side of body; $500+. *Susan Stanton-Reid Collection.*

Paddington Bear: 10" ca. 1980; plush; unjointed; felt toggle coat and hat; vinyl boots; made by Eden; hang tag; $65-$75.

Misha Bear: 17" 1984; made by Dakin for the Moscow Olympics; plush; wears Olympic rings belt; $100-$140

English Nisbet Bear: 17" ca. 1982; gold mohair; plastic eyes; velour pads; soft stuffed; made to honor Peter Bull; cloth label and "Bully Bear" hang tag; $150-$175.

Steiff *Mama* and *Baby*: 6" and 14", 1981; the second collector bear product; held together with ribbon; M.I. B. with certificate; $550+.

Gebr. Hermann Bear and Panda: 10" and 11", 1980s; mohair; plastic eyes; labels and hang tags; $150-$200. *Susan Stanton-Reid Collection.*

American Dakin Bear: 21"
1982; white wool; plastic
eyes; red and white striped
socks and muffler; leather tag
on chest; paper hang tag behind ear; label in back seam;
$150-$175.

English Canterbury *Dressing
Gown* Bear: 17" ca. 1985; tan
wool; plastic eyes; wears robe
of the same fabric; label in
back seam; hang tag; $250-
$275.

English Merrythought
Cheeky Bear: 11" ca. 1985;
blue plush; plastic eyes; bells
in ears; label on foot; hang
tag; $125-$135. *Susan
Stanton-Reid Collection.*

Hallie and *Cyrus*: 33"
1984-1989; issued with
different furs and clothes;
limited edition of 50; price
at issue $1,600.
Young Black Bear: 22"
1986-1990; issue price
$596.
Kate and *Jeffrey*: 22" 1988-
1989; issue price $792;
made by Beaver Valley.
Courtesy of Beaver Valley.

Hallie and *Cyrus*: 33" 1984-1990.
Merryweather and *Jed*: 24" 1984- 1985 made by Beaver Valley
in limited editions; the majority of Kaylee and Jeff's bears are
poseable with lock-line construction; have hand cast resin eyes,
noses and claws, and hinged mouths; wooden armatures;
$1,950 and $1,150. *Courtesy of Beaver Valley.*

Steiff *Margaret Strong Bear*: 20" 1986; white mohair; leather
pads; largest of four sizes; ltd. ed. of 750; brass button; hang
tag; $1,400+.

English Merrythought *Highlander Bear.* 36" 1986; gold mohair head and paws; plastic eyes; beautifully dressed; ltd. production; label on foot; $1400+. *Susan Stanton-Reid Collection.*

English Nisbet *Delicatessen Bear.* 24" 1987; pale gold mohair with patches to re-create Peter Bull's bear used in the movie "Brideshead Revisited"; issued with British Airways flight bag; label and hang tag; $500+.

Nisbet *Bully Bear,* 15" 1980s; gold mohair; plastic eyes; wears Peter Bull's signature sweater; label and hang tag; $300+.

Nisbet *Zodiac Bear.* 13" 1980s; cinnamon mohair; plastic eyes; wears apron and chef's hat; represents Taurus; label and hang tag; $95-$125; *Susan Stanton-Reid Collection.*

Lifesize Pooh: 18" 1986-1987; by R. John Wright; ltd. ed. of 2,500; tagged; © W. Disney; $1,400+.

Carrousel *Teddy Snowbird*: 13" 1988; made by Doris and Terry Michaud for the 1st Disney World convention; signed on foot; label in back seam; presentation box; $450-$475. *Susan Stanton-Reid Collection.*

R. John Wright Pooh: 14" 1988; ltd. edition made for the first Disney World convention; green ribbon with gold printing; © Disney; $1,295+.

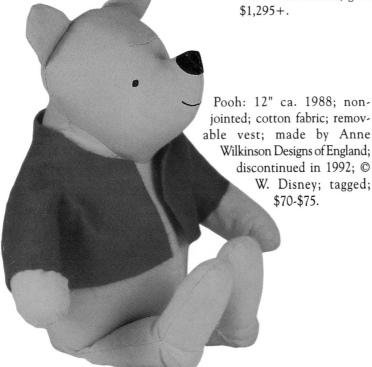

Pooh: 12" ca. 1988; non-jointed; cotton fabric; removable vest; made by Anne Wilkinson Designs of England; discontinued in 1992; © W. Disney; tagged; $70-$75.

Pooh in Chair: 10" 1989; made by R. John Wright for the 2nd Disney World convention; © Disney; tagged and signed on chair; $1,500+.

Beaver Valley *Winifred* and *Max*. 22" 1989-1991; ltd. ed. of 50 each; $575 each. *Courtesy of Beaver Valley.*

Beaver Valley *Young Black Bear*. 22" 1986-1990; ltd. ed. 500; $750. *Courtesy of Beaver Valley.*

Beaver Valley *Zoe* and *Oliver:* 22" 1989-1990; ltd. edition of 50; issue price $575; *Max* and *Winifred* described on previous page. *Courtesy of Beaver Valley.*

Artist Bear: 12" ca. 1990; made by Sue Foskey; mohair; distressed to look old; label; $250+. *Alice Channing Collection.*

Porridge Bear: 16" ca. 1982; tan woolly plush; plastic eyes; cotton shirt; reproduced by Dean's to emulate the advertising bear drawn by Jessie Wilcox Smith; ltd. to 7,500; sewn-in label; two hang tags; presentation box; $350-$375. Campbell Soup Advertising Bear: 13" © 1995; cotton plush; plastic eyes; ltd. ed. of 2,400; labels on feet and back; hang tag; presentation box; issue price $89.95. *Susan Stanton-Reid Collec-*

Antiqued Teddy: 10" 1990; made to emulate early American Bear; antiqued with dyes; one of a kind by Jon Van Houten; $150 at issue.

Papa Bear: 6" 1992; muslin, cotton, and ultra suede; made by Gladys Boalt; $50-$60.

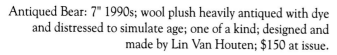

Antiqued Bear: 7" 1990s; wool plush heavily antiqued with dye and distressed to simulate age; one of a kind; designed and made by Lin Van Houten; $150 at issue.

Beaver Valley *Zoe* and *Oliver:* 22" 1989-1990; ltd. edition of 50; issue price $575; *Max* and *Winifred* described on previous page. *Courtesy of Beaver Valley.*

Artist Bear: 12" ca. 1990; made by Sue Foskey; mohair; distressed to look old; label; $250+. *Alice Channing Collection.*

Porridge Bear: 16" ca. 1982; tan woolly plush; plastic eyes; cotton shirt; reproduced by Dean's to emulate the advertising bear drawn by Jessie Wilcox Smith; ltd. to 7,500; sewn-in label; two hang tags; presentation box; $350-$375. Campbell Soup Advertising Bear: 13" © 1995; cotton plush; plastic eyes; ltd. ed. of 2,400; labels on feet and back; hang tag; presentation box; issue price $89.95. *Susan Stanton-Reid Collec-*

German Gebr. Hermann Bear: 16"; made to commemorate the unification of Germany, October 1990; ltd. ed. of 4,000; label in seam; button on back of head; plastic and paper hang tags; $400-$450.

Little Brown Bear: 13" 1987; produced to emulate the bear in the book of the same title by Johnny Gruelle; made by Nisbet, England; 1,000 made; with booklet; $250-$300. *Bonnie and Larry Vaughan Collection.*

Artist Bear: 10" ca. 1990; made by Sue Foskey to look old and worn; $150-$175. *Alice Channing Collection.*

Gebr. Hermann Bear: 11.50" ca. 1990; mohair; plastic eyes; carries a Christmas tree, wears a scarf; comes on wooden stand; label and paper logo on tree bottom; $175-$200. *Susan Stanton-Reid Collection.*

Dreamkid Bear: 10" 1990s; by Heidi Ott; rubber; bean bag filled body; one of several styles; hang tag; M. I. B; $35-$40.

Hermann Spielwaren Bears: 12", 15" and 20"; 1990s; mohair; plastic eyes; inset muzzles; Tyrolean clothes; dress not issued with 20" bear; ltd. editions; labels; embroidered feet on two largest; $175-$225. *Susan Stanton-Reid Collection.*

Paddington Bears: 14" and 20" 1990s; made by Gabrielle, England; $130-$150. *Courtesy of Gabrielle Designs Ltd.*

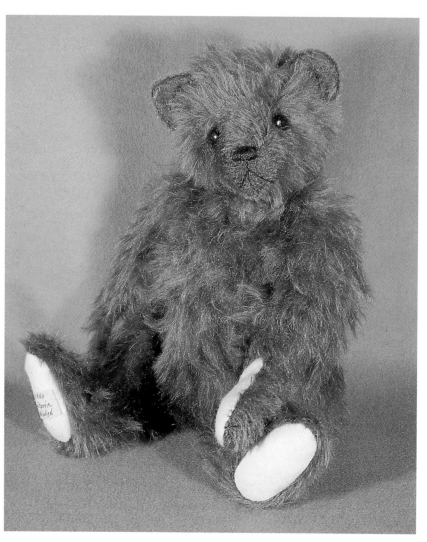

Traditional Bear: 18" 1990s; brown mohair; one of a kind; by artist Lin Van Houten; $250 issue price.

Beaver Valley *Ian* and *Ursula*: 25" 1991; Boy ltd. ed. of 25; $1,300; Grizzly ltd. ed. of 50; $1,200. *Courtesy of Beaver Valley.*

Carol Stewart Pooh: 5.50" 1991; made by the artist in a limited edition of 100 for the Disney World Convention; sold with enamel pin; signed; $425-$450.

Sitting Panda: 6.50" 1990s; wool plush; designed and made by Lin and Jon Van Houten; $160 issue price.

Artist Bear: 12.50" 1992; prototype of the bear made in a limited edition of 25 for the convention at Disneyland by Jeanette Warner; wears a vest, Mickey Mouse pen, and carries an autograph book; sold for $165 at issue.

Bear on Fours: 13" 1990s; hand-stitched mohair distressed by artist; fully jointed (unusual for this pattern); resembles early toy; one of a kind; by artist Jon Van Houten; $240 at issue.

Beaver Valley *Josie*: 14" 1991-1992; ltd. ed. of 100; $280. *Courtesy of Beaver Valley.*

Beaver Valley *Blackburn*: 17" 1991-1993; ltd. ed. of 100; $575. *Courtesy of Beaver Valley.*

Disney Bear; plush bear made as a logo for the first Disneyland Convention in 1992; © Disney; $40-$50.

Antiqued Teddy: 10" 1990; made to emulate early American Bear; antiqued with dyes; one of a kind by Jon Van Houten; $150 at issue.

Papa Bear: 6" 1992; muslin, cotton, and ultra suede; made by Gladys Boalt; $50-$60.

Antiqued Bear: 7" 1990s; wool plush heavily antiqued with dye and distressed to simulate age; one of a kind; designed and made by Lin Van Houten; $150 at issue.

Pooh: 12" 1993; made by Carrousel for the Disney World Convention; ltd. ed. of 100; wears nightshirt and cap; M. I. B; $475+.

Pooh type Bear: 14" 1990s; designed to resemble 1920s bear; loose joints; heavily antiqued; wool jacket; by Lin Van Houten; $200 at issue.

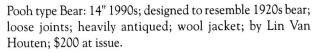

Animated *Gift Giver*: 36" 1993; made from an antique Russian lap robe; long mohair beard; carrying gifts; one of a kind; by artist Christina Wemmit-Pauk; $2,500 issue price.

Animated Le Biker: 18" 1993; ltd. ed. of 25; mohair; dressed in wool with lace and brass stars as trim; an auction piece for the "In Time For Peace" benefit with friends of the French Embassy in Washington, D.C.; by artist Christina Wemmit-Pauk; $425 issue price.

German Gebr. Hermann Bear: 8" ca. 1994; tipped mohair; plastic eyes; ltd. ed. of 1,000; plastic and paper hang tags and certificate; $100-$125.

Huckleberry Finn: 18" 1993; Robert Raikes design produced by Applause; ltd. ed. of 5,000; signed and numbered; $275. *Susan Stanton-Reid Collection.*

English Gabrielle Pooh and Piglet: 10" and 6"; ltd. edition; 1994; imaginatively boxed to emulate Pooh Stick Bridge; © Disney; $250-$300

Steiff "Opera" Bear; made in 1994 for Harrod's, London; wears velvet cloak and has a wind-up music box that plays "All I Ask of You" from Phantom of The Opera; M. I. B; limited edition; $500-$550.

Steiff Teddy Baby Bears: 9"; given to the group of nine who visited Giengen in September 1994; enhanced by satin ribbons signed by Mr. Juninger; no price available.

English Gabrielle Pooh: 11" 1994; mohair; knit vest; ltd. ed. of 2,000; presentation box, "hunny" pot and certificates; © W. Disney; $175-$200.

Steiff *Pooh* Bear: 12" 1994; made in a ltd. ed. of 2,500 for the Disney World Convention; © Disney; $600+.

English Gabrielle Pooh: 10" 1995; comes in presentation box with table, chair, and tablecloth; box represents a kitchen; this is in conjunction with Royal Doulton and also includes a Royal Doulton plate, mug and clock; classic Pooh figures on the china; M. I. B; © W. Disney; $250 (approximately) at issue.

German Gebr. Hermann Bear: 12" 1994; ltd. ed. of 100 pieces for the Doll and Toy Museum in Rothenburg, Germany; data embroidered on felt apron; plastic hang tag and certificate; $250-$300.

Jingles: 18" 1995; open edition; a church baby whose mohair is antiqued; brass bells around the neck; made by artist Christina Wemmit-Pauk; $225 issue price.

Yes, Matthew There Are Leprechauns In Ireland; 1995; one of a kind sculpture; face of German clay; poseable mohair body; by artist Christina Wemmit-Pauk; $595 issue price.

Paddington Bear: 13" 1995; ltd. ed. of 5,000; made by Gabrielle Designs; beautiful presentation box; $325. *Courtesy of Gabrielle Designs Ltd.*

Pooh's Tree House: 28" 1995; tree house featuring Pooh, Piglet, Eeyore, Kanga/Roo and Tigger; made by Gabrielle Designs exclusively for Theodore's Teddy Shop in London; $375 at issue. *Courtesy of Gabrielle Designs Ltd.*

Aunt Lucy: 14" 1995; ltd. ed. of 2,000; made by Gabrielle Designs; Paddington's Peruvian Aunt is also presented in a beautiful and imaginative box; $325. *Courtesy of Gabrielle Designs Ltd.*

Animated *Elfin*: 18" 1995; ltd. ed. of 5; holds lighted candle; by artist Christina Wemmit-Pauk; $495 issue price.

Animated *Renaissance Angel*: 18" 1995; ltd. ed. of ten; mohair bear dressed in 100 year old French lace; wings composed and antiqued by artist; lighted candle head piece; made by artist Christina Wemmit-Pauk; $495 issue price.

Right: Steiff *Baloo* Bear: 15" 1995; made in a ltd. ed. of 2,500 for the Disney World Convention; a © W. Disney item from the Jungle Book cartoon feature; brass button and chest tag; price at issue $300; secondary market evaluation not determined at time of writing.

Bottom Right: Artist Angel Bears: 12" 1995; made by author; top bear sold with the harp; $250 at issue each.

Below: Artist Bear: 19" 1990s; expressive teddy by Canadian artist Donna McPherson; $160 at issue.

Artist Bear 21" 1990s; wearing vintage clothes and accompanied by photo of children of the same period; by Canadian artist Donna McPherson; $225 at issue.

Artist Bears: 22" 1990s; award winning designs by Canadian artist Donna McPherson; fashioned from antique sleigh blankets and with old shoe buttons for eyes; $175-$195 at issue.

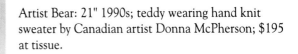

Artist Bear: 21" 1990s; teddy wearing hand knit sweater by Canadian artist Donna McPherson; $195 at tissue.

Barefoot Teddy: 24" 1995; "Mary Ann" by artist Gloria Franks; carries rag doll; tagged and signed; gift to author.

Sam Bear: 16" 1995; designed by Salley Winey for Ty Inc; unjointed; plush; hang tag on ear; signed on foot; $25-$30.

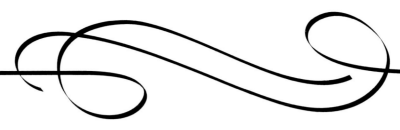

CHAPTER VII
A BEAR OF A DIFFERENT COLOR

Rhett Beartler:
20" 1980s; blue ve-
lour; imaginatively
dressed; non-jointed;
made by North American
Bears; label; $125-

German Wilhelm Strunz Bear: 15" ca. 1907; blond mohair head, paws, and feet; shoe button eyes; black embroidered nose and claws; red embroidered mouth; costume forms the body; pin jointed limbs visible from the outside; no ID; $2,800-$3,200.

American Bear: 15" ca. 1908; gold mohair head, lower arms and legs; four color linen body; glass eyes; ruffs and trim added; no ID; $750-$850.

French Clown Bear: 13.50" ca. 1908; tan coat wool head, paws and feet; glass eyes; gutta percha nose; colorful plush forms the body; felt ruffs; no ID; $2,500-$3,000.

German Jester Bear: 16" ca. 1910; white mohair head, paws and feet; green and pink plush forms the body suit and hat; shoe button eyes; no ID; sold at Christie's South Kensington, London in 1995 for approximately $6,500; shown with Steiff Skittles. *Courtesy of Christie's, London.*

American Bear: 22" ca. 1908; red mohair; non-working electric eye bear; glass eyes replace light bulbs; battery pack removed; tie not original; no ID; $200-$300.

American Patriotic Bears: 20" ca. 1912; red, white, and blue mohair; glass eyes; jointed arms; original silk ribbon on the bear to the right; no ID; $850+ each. *Susan Stanton-Reid Collection.*

Steiff Bear Dolly: 12" 1913; white mohair head; red mohair body and limbs; shoe button eyes; white yarn ruff; introduced at the Leipzig Toy Fair; printed button; sold at Christie's South Kensington, London in 1994 for approximately $16,625. *Courtesy of Christie's, London.*

Steiff Bear: 15" made in 1912 for the English market only; rare since only 494 were produced in this curly black mohair; shoe button eyes backed by red felt; no ID; sold in 1994 at Christie's South Kensington, London for approximately $6,200. *Courtesy of Christie's, London.*

Steiff Bear: 20" 1912; black curly mohair; shoe button eyes; sold at Christie's South Kensington, London in 1994 for approximately $35,000. *Courtesy of Christie's, London.*

English Steevans Bear; 12" ca. 1918; rose mohair; shoe button eyes; musical chimes encased in body; metal button in left ear marked "Steevans England P T 12 6846"; company in business for a few years only; sold in 1994 at Christie's South Kensington, London for approximately $2,800. *Courtesy of Christie's, London.*

English Merrythought Bear: 19" ca. 1930; lime green silk plush; green felt paw pads; label on foot; $1,500-$1,600.

Schuco Perfume Bear: 5" ca. 1925; dark red mohair over metal; metal bead eyes; head lifts off to reveal a glass scent bottle with stopper; no ID; $875-$900.

Musical Bear: 16" ca. 1920; cream mohair with red tipping; glass eyes; internal squeeze-type music box; appears to be made by Jopi; no ID; sold at Christie's, London in December 1995 for approximately $1,675. Musical Bear: 17" ca. 1930; pale green faded mohair; glass eyes; music movement in the head activated by tilting the bear back and forth; one eye missing; made by Crämer; no ID; sold at Christie's, London in December 1995 for approximately $1,325. *Courtesy of Christie's, London.*

169

English Bear: 21" ca 1930; pink mohair; glass eyes; kapok stuffed; no ID; $900-$950.

German Jopi Bellows Music Box Bear: 14" 1930s; orangey frosted mohair; glass eyes; no ID; $3,000+. *Courtesy of David Douglass.*

English Nisbet Coronation Bear: 14" 1977; one of a kind to celebrate the Queen's Silver Jubilee; black alpaca; wears replica of the Queen's tabard; the actual issue was gold mohair; tag signed by Jack Wilson, company director; $350+.
English Nisbet *Paddy The Irishman* Bear: 15" ca. 1975 prototype; tag on foot; hang tag; $350-$370; both bears are from the Nisbet Archives. *Susan Stanton-Reid Collection.*

Above: English Chiltern Skater Bear: 11" ca. 1935; gold silky head and lower body; pink and white plush arms, upper torso, muff and hood; glass eyes; pillbox hat holds a squeaker; kapok stuffed; label on foot; sold in 1994 at Christie's South Kensington, London; for approximately $425. *Courtesy of Christie's, London.*

Top Right: English Chiltern Bear: 19" ca. 1938; pink mohair; glass eyes; no ID; $900-$1,000.

English Farnell Bear: 18" ca. 1930; black mohair; glass eyes; kapok stuffed; no ID; $1,300-$1,400.

Schuco Yes/No Bear: 20" ca. 1930; bright blue mohair; glass eyes; growler; no ID; sold at Christie's South Kensington, London for approximately $9,625.
Schuco Yes/No Bear: 21" ca. 1950; tan mohair; glass eyes; no ID; sold at Christie's for approximately $975. *Courtesy of Christie's, London.*

Dean's *Tru-To-Life* Bear: 22" ca. 1950; black plush; inset muzzle; internal rubber mask that formed sockets when the glass eyes were attached; molded nose; rubber foot pads and claws; label on leg; sold in 1995 at Christie's, London for approximately $5,625. *Courtesy of Christie's, London.*

American Bear: 13" ca. 1940; pink cotton string plush; glass eyes; no ID; $100-$150.

Steiff Club Bear: 13" 1994; replica of *Elliot*; available to Steiff Club members only; price at issue $225; will double in price on the secondary market.

Above: William Shakesbear: 20" 1980s; burgundy velour; plastic eyes; non-jointed; velvet satin and felt clothes; made by North American Bears; label on foot; $150-$175.

Steiff Replica Alfonzo: 13" 1990; red mohair; satin Cossack; produced by Steiff for Ian Pout for his shop in England in a limited edition of 5,000; Ian purchased the original bear at auction; Alfonzo has a Russian provenance; M. I. B; $550+.

Steiff Bear *Elliot*: 13" ca. 1908; blue mohair; one of a kind made as a sample for Harrod's Dept. Store; auctioned at Christie's, London in 1993 for approximately $74,250. *Courtesy of Christie's, London.*

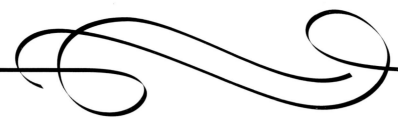

CHAPTER VIII
PALS

Steiff Bear: 30" ca.
1910' white mohair;
shoe button eyes; no
ID; $5,000-$6,000;
with "Pooh Bear" cat.

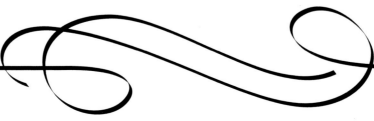

E. I. Horsman Billiken Bear: 12" 1909; tan mohair; composition head; jointed limbs; sewn on label; $500-$600. American Ideal Bear: 13" ca. 1908; gold mohair; shoe button eyes; no ID; $1,000-$1,200.

Steiff Bear: 24" ca. 1907; apricot mohair; shoe button eyes; center head seam; printed button; $6,500-$7,000; with Schuco Mickey Mouse.

English Farnell Nightdress Case: 13" ca. 1950; gold mohair; glass eyes; zipper opening; sewn on label; $375-$400; with Steiff cocker spaniel.

Steiff Bear: 12" ca. 1910; white mohair; glass eyes; printed button; $1,700-$1,800; with Steiff chicken.

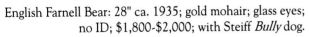

English Farnell Bear: 28" ca. 1935; gold mohair; glass eyes; no ID; $1,800-$2,000; with Steiff *Bully* dog.

American Bear on Wheels: 13" ca. 1910; cinnamon mohair; glass eyes; cast iron wheels; wire muzzle and chain; no I.D; $800-$850.

Schuco Yes/No Bellhop Bear: 10.50" ca. 1925; gold mohair; shoe button eyes; felt suit forms body; no ID; $3,000-$3,400.

Schuco Perfume Bear: 5" ca. 1925; pink mohair over metal; head lifts off to reveal bottle and stopper; no ID; $800-$900; with Schuco mechanical rabbit.

R. John Wright *Michael And His Teddy*: ltd. ed. of 250 pieces in the 1980s; M. I. B. $1,000-$1,200; with two Steiff dogs.

German Bing Bear: 27" ca. 1925; gold mohair; glass eyes; no ID; $3,900-$4,200; with "Victoria."

Steiff Teddy Baby: 12" ca. 1930; blond mohair; glass eyes; clothes not original to bear; printed button; $2,500-$3,000; with artist doll.

The Three Bears Puzzle: 13" x 18"; ca. 1920;
Who's been sitting in my chair? Numbered 4318;
$100-$125.

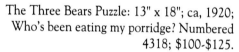

The Three Bears Puzzle: 13" x 18"; ca, 1920;
Who's been eating my porridge? Numbered
4318; $100-$125.

The Three Bears Puzzle: 13" x 18"; ca. 1920;
Who's been sleeping in my bed? Numbered
4318; $100-$125.

R. John Wright *Michael And His Teddy*: ltd. ed. of 250 pieces in the 1980s; M. I. B. $1,000-$1,200; with two Steiff dogs.

German Bing Bear: 27" ca. 1925; gold mohair; glass eyes; no ID; $3,900-$4,200; with "Victoria."

Steiff Teddy Baby: 12" ca. 1930; blond mohair; glass eyes; clothes not original to bear; printed button; $2,500-$3,000; with artist doll.

Steiff Bear: 17" ca. 1925; gold mohair; glass eyes; printed button; clothes not original; $2,500-$3,000; with Steiff donkey.

Steiff Bear: 13" ca. 1930; faded mohair showing pink in unexposed to light areas; glass eyes; ruff not original; printed button; $1,000-$1,200; with Steiff *Fluffy* cat.

Schuco Yes/No Bear: 13"
ca. 1948; tan mohair;
glass eyes; original dress;
no ID; $950-$1,050; with
Steiff rabbit.

Steiff Bear: 24" ca. 1910;
white mohair; shoe button
eyes; printed button;
$6,500-$7,500; with Steiff
Mickey Mouse puppet and
plush Mickey.

Steiff Cosy Teddy: 16" ca.
1958; white dralon; tan
chest plate; glass eyes;
chest tag; $175-$185; with
English Golliwogg.

Steiff Standing Bear: 22" ca. 1965; tan mohair; glass eyes; wheels removed; no ID; $650-$700; with "Albert."

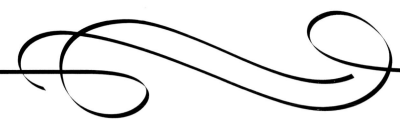

CHAPTER IX
NOT QUITE TEDDIES

Chain saw carved bear: 24", that greets visitors at the end of our driveway.

Carved wooden toilet tissue holder: 9.50" ca. 1920; no ID; $225-$250.

Wooden Wagon: 20" 1988-1989; Advertising Beary Bros. soap; made as a replica by Bartholomew Co. of California; ID hand marked on the bottom; $500-$550.

Wooden plaque: 18" ca. 1907; wood burned; American; Flemish Art Co/938/New York; $85-$95.

Illustration from *The Wonderful Story of Teddy The Bear*, note how the hunter resembles Teddy Roosevelt.

"Shake hands, young feller."

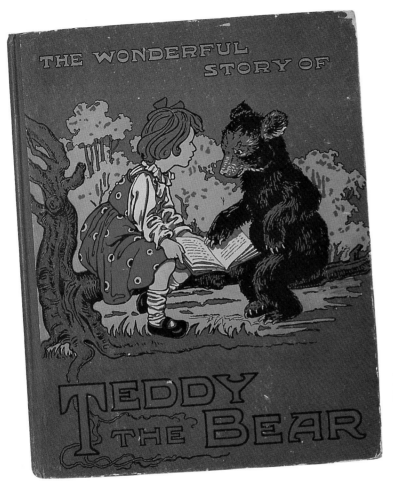

Book: *The Wonderful Story of Teddy The Bear*, 1907; by Sarah Noble-Ives; $225-$250.

The Traveling Bears Books: © 1915 by Barse and Hopkins; two in a series of ten condensed from the four larger volumes of the Roosevelt Bears; by Seymour Eaton. $100-$125.

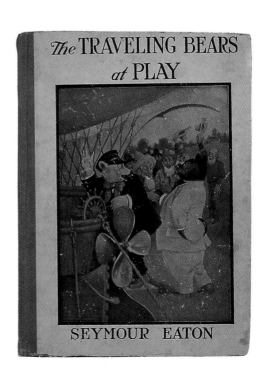

185

Advertising Book: ca. 1920; *The Union Pacific Children's Book of Yellowstone Bears*; tale of bears who enjoy the comfort of the railroad. $125-$130.

Figural Christmas card booklet; 1929; $25-$35.

Mechanical walker: 8.50" ca. 1935; papier maché head; cotton clothes over wire; key wound; no ID; $100-$125.
Metal walker: 4.75" ca. 1950; made by Chien; U S A; $75-$85.

Figural Bear pitcher: 5" ca. 1910; bear's mouth is pour spout; made by Shafer Vater; Germany; no ID; $185-$225.

German Zoo: 17" ca. 1920; wire cage; molded caves; elastolin polar bears; no ID; $500-$550.

Print: 13" ca. 1917; entitled "A Soldier And His Girl," no ID; possibly English; $125-$150.

Royal Doulton figurine: 7.50" 1982; Childhood Days-And So To Bed; $250-$295.

Fabric Teddy Bear; when cut, sewn and stuffed makes a 22" and two 5" bears; 1913; Saalfield Publishing Co; instructions printed on the cloth; $295-$325.

Roosevelt Bears Post cards; 1906-1907 illustrations from Seymour Eaton's books; E. Stern and Co. $40-$45 each.

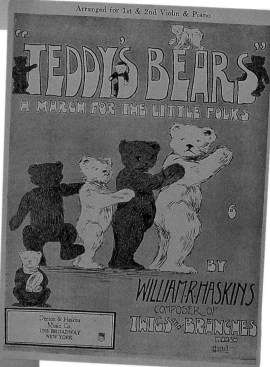

Sheet Music; "Teddy's Bears"; 1925; "A March For Little Folks"; William R. Haskins; $40-$45.

Mother Goose's Teddy Bear Post cards; 1907; from the book by Frederick L. Cavally Jr. $30-$35 each.

The Three Bears Puzzle: 13" x 18"; ca. 1920; Who's been sitting in my chair? Numbered 4318; $100-$125.

The Three Bears Puzzle: 13" x 18"; ca, 1920; Who's been eating my porridge? Numbered 4318; $100-$125.

The Three Bears Puzzle: 13" x 18"; ca. 1920; Who's been sleeping in my bed? Numbered 4318; $100-$125.

Figurine: 3" 1995; made especially for The Teddy Bear Reunion In The Heartland in Clarion, Iowa; The Boyds collection. $200+.

Figurine: 2" 1992; made by Peter Fagan for Harrod's Dept. Store, London; Scotland; $45-$50.

Advertising stick pin: ca. 1907; advertisement for Teddy Bear Bread; printed information on brass backing; $195+.

Brass Bank: 6" ca. 1900; no ID; $125-$150.

Tin Candy Mold: 8" ca. 1900; European; marked 40 1/2 1309; $325-$350.

Metal Inkwell: 4"
ca. 1900; glass in-
sert for ink; no ID;
$175-$200.

Baer Family Re-
union Pin Back
Button: 2.25";
seventh annual
reunion of the
family held at
Kutztown Park
in 1906; one in
a series; ID. on
reverse; The
Weber badge
and Novelty Co.
Reading Pa. $80-
$85.

Santa Candy containers: 5.25"; made by artist Jeanette Warner in 1994; pulls apart at middle to reveal cardboard container; $155 at issue.

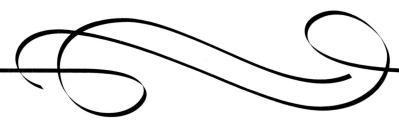

CHAPTER X
HOLIDAY HAPPENINGS

Holiday Cheer;
Steiff Bear: 24"
ca. 1907;
$6,500-$7,500.

Toasting In The New Year: Steiff Bear: 24" ca. 1925; $4,000-$5,000; Steiff Bear; 24"; ca. 1910; $6,500-$7,500.

Valentine Greetings; American Bear: 24" ca. 1910; $2,000+.

The Wearing Of The Green; American Aetna Bear: 20" ca. 1907; $1,450-$1,550.
Steiff Bear: 24" ca. 1905; $7,500-$8,500.

Three Cheers For The Red, White And Blue On Memorial
Day; American Ideal 20" Bear ca. 1908; $1,200-$1,300.

Old Glory On July 4th; Steiff Bear: 29" ca. 1910; $5,000-
$6,000.

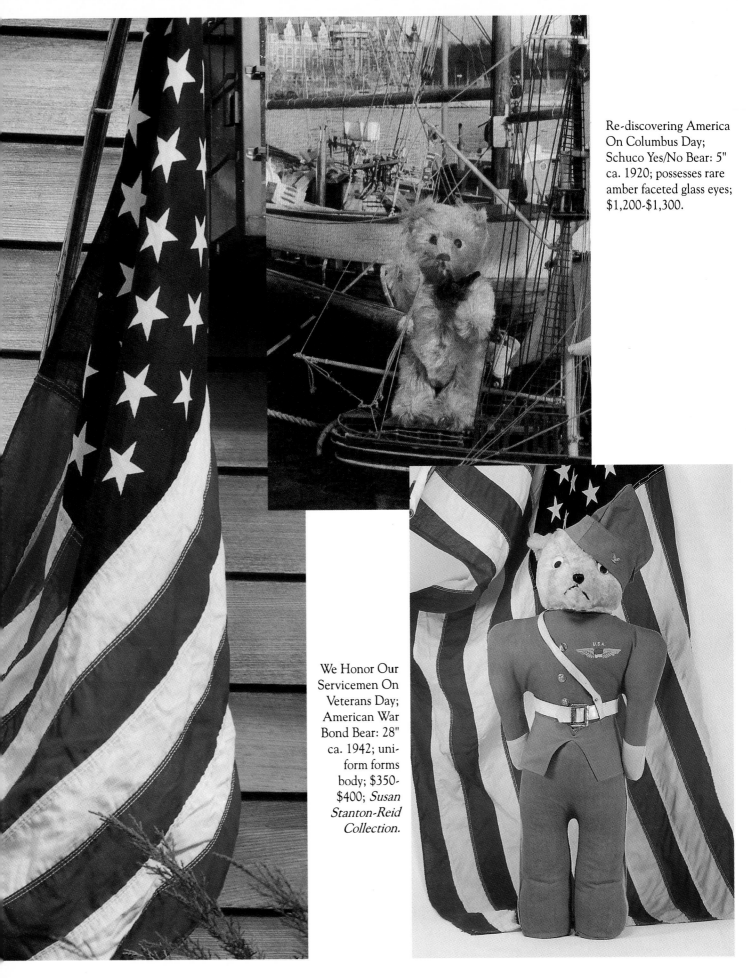

Re-discovering America
On Columbus Day;
Schuco Yes/No Bear: 5"
ca. 1920; possesses rare
amber faceted glass eyes;
$1,200-$1,300.

We Honor Our
Servicemen On
Veterans Day;
American War
Bond Bear: 28"
ca. 1942; uni-
form forms
body; $350-
$400; *Susan
Stanton-Reid
Collection.*

Bringing Home The Great Pumpkin; Steiff Bear: 24" ca. 1905; $7,500-$8,500.

Pass The Turkey; American Bear: 16" ca. 1907; $1,400-$1,500.

Gathering Christmas Greens; Steiff Bear: 24" ca. 1907; $6,500-$7,500.

Post card Santa: 12.50" 1994; made by artist Jeanette Warner to emulate the 1907 post card; $165 at issue.

The Perfect Christmas Face; Steiff Bear: 20" ca. 1905; $7,500.

Trimming The Teddy Tree; Steiff Bear: 12" ca. 1910; $1,500-$1,600; Schuco Bear: 12" ca. 1950; $1,000-$1,100; Steiff Bear: 3.50" ca. 1950; $295-$325.

The Joys Of Christmas; Steiff Bears: 30", 24", 16", ca. 1910; $1,500-$7,500.

Cookies And Milk For Santa; Steiff Bear: 12" ca. 1910; $1,600.

Santa Himself; by artist Barbara Connley; 1980; no price available.

Opposite Page: Good Night Beautiful Tree; Steiff Bear: 24" ca. 1910; $6,500-$7,500.

INDEX

ABOUT THE AUTHOR

Dee Hockenberry lives in a small town in western New York with her husband, Tom, who photographs all of her work. They share their cottage in the woods with three cats, a den of Teddy Bears, and many other toys and related memorabilia. Dee and Tom are the parents of two grown children.

Dee began her career as a Teddy Bear designer and still supplies selected shops as far away as Singapore. She is the author of seven other collectible books and is also a regular contributor to three Teddy Bear magazines; two in the U. S. and one in England. She is recognized internationally in the world of bears and Steiff animals, often lecturing on the subject. Along with a partner she operates a mail order business selling Steiff and other soft toys and accessories and may be seen at several shows and sales each year.